THE CHRISTIAN
COUNSELING MANUAL

THE CHRISTIAN COUNSELING MANUAL

Techniques and Practices to Reclaim Godly Mental Health

Jenee' Q. Landrum, PhD

JenVa Publishing

Copyright©2020 by JenVa Publishing

All rights reserved. No part of this book may be reproduced in any form
or by any electronic or mechanical means, including information storage
and retrieval systems, without permission in writing from the publisher,
except by a reviewer who may quote brief passages in a review.

Library of Congress Cataloging-in- Publication Data
on file

ISBN: 978-1-7379914-5-8

Second Edition Reissued 2021

Printed in the United States of America

Published in New Orleans, Louisiana by JenVa Publishing

Table of Contents

Introduction

The world is experiencing increasing instability, and many are struggling to cope. In attempts to manage, individuals are seeking relief from a multitude of distinctive and occasionally unhealthy courses. Fortunately, Christian Counseling is emerging as an important means of both spiritual and mental health support.

Many established authorities have come to recognize the powerful holistic advantages of Christian Counseling in assisting in the healing process. This recognition has led to increased education and training for those seeking to practice as Christian Counselors. As well as increased opportunities for clergy practicing in this area to become more skillful in aiding parishioners.

This Manual is designed as a companion to those engaged in or studying the practice of Christian Counseling. It covers many common conditions and highlights areas where preventative measures may be of great benefit. It also accentuates disorders that are more distinct.

Regardless of denominational leaning or lack thereof, the Christian Counseling Manual is a guide into the personal struggles plaguing individuals, and the effects those struggles can have on their daily lives and those in close proximity. It provides practical definitions, techniques and resources that benefit counselor and counselee alike as together they reclaim the territory of godly mental health.

The Lord is near to those with a broken heart and saves those with a contrite spirit. Many are the afflictions of the righteous, but the Lord delivers him out of them all.
(Psalm 34:18-19)

SECTION I

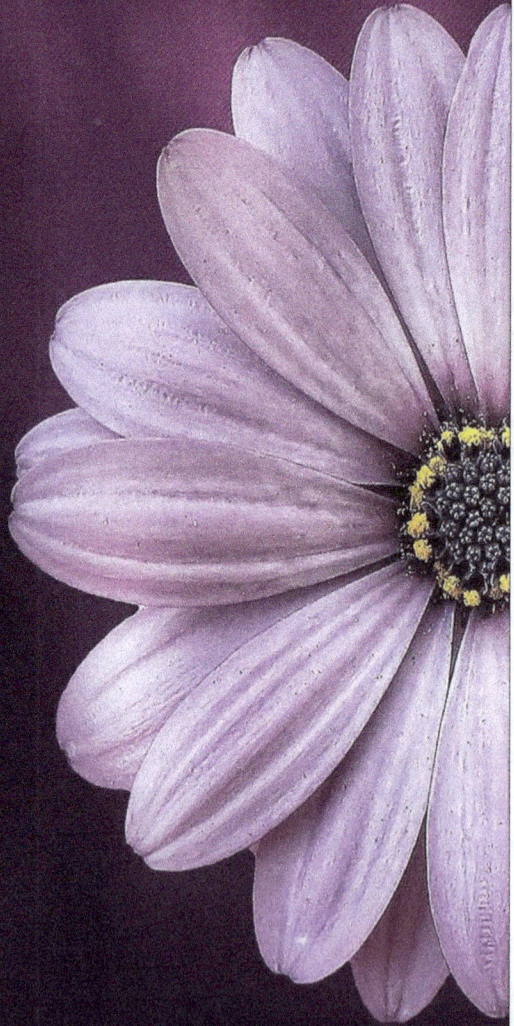

ANXIETY

Anxiety is the inner feeling of apprehension, uneasiness, worry and or dread that is accompanied by a heightened physical arousal.

Anxiety is a normal and often healthy emotion. It warns people of danger and motivates them to act. However, when a person regularly feels disproportionate levels of *Anxiety*, it can become a mental and or physical disorder; creating panic and even immobilizing individuals. *Anxiety* disorders form a category of mental health diagnoses, that lead to excessive nervousness, fear, apprehension, and worry. In times of high or chronic anxiety, the body becomes remarkably "on alert" and can create actual physical harm.

Psychological symptoms of Anxiety may include feelings of fear and dread, an exaggerated startle reflex, poor concentration, irritability, and insomnia. Additionally, cognitive disturbances such as hyper-vigilance, racing thoughts, or unwanted thoughts are common.

Physical symptoms of Anxiety include shortness of breath, racing heart, fatigue, sweating, restlessness/ insomnia, muscle aches, GI distress and immune system depression resulting in chronic colds and infections.

In mild to moderate Anxiety, a surge in the hormone adrenaline (epinephrine) gives rise to symptoms such as tremor, perspiration, and muscle tension.

In severe Anxiety, hyperventilation (over-breathing) can lead to a fall in the concentration of carbon dioxide in the blood. This gives rise to an additional set of physical symptoms, among which chest discomfort, numbness or tingling in the hands and feet, dizziness, and faintness.

The psychological and physical symptoms of Anxiety vary according to the nature and magnitude of the perceived threat, and from one person to another.

For Spiritual Support:

Be careful for nothing; but in everything by prayer and supplication with thanksgiving let your requests be made know unto God.

And the peace of God, which passeth all understanding, shall keep your hearts and minds through Christ Jesus.

Finally, brethren, whatsoever things are true, whatsoever things are honest, whatsoever things are just, whatsoever things pure, whatsoever things are lovely, whatsoever things are of good report if there be any virtue, and if there be any praise, think on these things.

Those things, which ye have both learned, and received and heard, and seen in me, do: and the God of peace shall be with you

Philippians 4:6-9

Wherefore I put thee in remembrance that thou stir up the gift of God which is in thee by the putting on of my hands.

For God has not given us the spirit of fear, but of power, and of love and of a sound mind

II Timothy 1:6-7

For they that are after the flesh do mind the things of the flesh; but they that are after the Spirit the things of the Spirit.
For to be carnally minded is death; but to be spiritually minded is life and peace.
Romans 8:5-6

9 Tips for Living with Anxiety

For many, living with Anxiety requires daily effort. Medication can be very effective in reducing distress, but it doesn't have to be your only treatment. Try these additional self- care techniques to help you calm your mind and reduce your stress.

Breathe deeply: Deep breathing signals to your brain that you're okay. Your brain then tells your mind and body to relax. For best results, lie flat on your back with one hand on your abdomen and the other on your chest. Then inhale slowly. Take in enough air to fill your belly and make it rise slightly. Hold for 2 seconds then exhale

Get Moving: Exercise. It's great for your mental and physical health. It relieves stress, releases chemicals in the brain that helps boost your mood and its physical results are great for a sense of overall well-being. Three to five 30-minute sessions a week will do the trick. Don't forget to choose an activity you like

Release Muscle Tension: The body can hold stress in the muscles. Release those muscles with this simple exercise. Focus on a muscle group, tighten them for a few seconds, then release. Repeat this process until you work through your entire body one section at a time.

Back off on the Caffeine and Alcohol: Both caffeine and alcohol can trigger your Anxiety. Though caffeine is a stimulant and alcohol is a depressant they both trigger changes in the body that can cause significant problems. So, avoid them altogether if you can. Do your best to say good-bye to them both be it in, soda, coffee, chocolate, tea, diet pills and even some headache meds.

Take Control of your thoughts: Make a deliberate effort to see "the glass as half full" instead of "half empty. Practice being positive. Also, mentally see yourself facing your fears head-on. This exercise allows your mind to grow accustomed to them and makes it easier to deal with real challenges when they appear

Schedule "Worry Time": This may seem strange, but doctors recommend that you take about 30 minutes a day to think about your fears, on purpose. The session should be at the time every day. This is not a time to drive yourself crazy with "what ifs", but a time to order your thoughts to focus on what really makes you anxious and what you can do about it.

Watch your sleep habits: Doctors recommend 8 hours of sleep every night. But the quality of that sleep just as important. If Anxiety is making it difficult to get consistent restful sleep, then create a routine that will help you.

Be sure your bed is comfortable
Keep your room on the cool side
Set a bedtime and stick to it
Turn off your screens (phones, tablets and TVs)

Be Conscious of Triggers: Take time to notice times or places where you feel most anxious. Look for patterns and work on ways to either avoid or even confront these feelings. Write them down if you need to. Recognizing causes of your Anxiety can help you find better perspective and be better prepared before something triggers you.

Help Others: Volunteer or do other work in your community. Spend time helping others and you'll spend less time in your own head. Giving back not only feels good but it nurtures relationships with others that can be supportive for you as well.

The Mind-Body Connection

Mood Food: Foods to Ease Anxiety

Anxiety is a mood disorder that effects millions of people every day. It starts in the brain. Your brain takes care of your thoughts and movements, your breathing and heartbeat, as well as your senses. It works 24/7, even while you're asleep. It requires a constant supply of fuel and that fuel comes from the foods you eat. What you eat directly affects the structure and function of your brain. Ultimately, that same fuel affects your mood.

With Anxiety, studies show that there's a clear relationship between the food you consume and your state of mind. A healthy diet is protective to the body and the mind, while an unhealthy diet can trigger feelings of anxiety and depression or worsen other mental health issues. Nutrients including omega-3 fatty acids, folic acid, vitamin D, magnesium, B vitamins, and tryptophan are vital in reinforcing stable moods, chemical health and a general feeling of emotional well-being. These are all found in foods that are part of a healthy diet.

As you manager your Anxiety, a lifestyle change that includes a diet high in vegetables, fruit, legumes, whole grains and lean protein will help you maintain a healthy state of mind. Combining eating

16

regularly, with foods that have a positive effect on your health and avoiding foods that don't, you'll now have meals that help you to feel better.

Foods to Help Reduce Anxiety

1.   Brazil Nuts

        Brazil Nuts are high in selenium. Selenium reduces inflammation, which is usually at high levels in those with mood disorders such as Anxiety. It's an antioxidant, which prevents cell damage. Antioxidants are beneficial in the treatment of Anxiety. Selenium is anti-carcinogenic, so it fights cancer too. In addition to brazil nuts, mushrooms and soybeans are also great sources of selenium. Brazil Nuts are high in Vitamin E another good source of antioxidants.

2.   Fatty Fish

        Omega-3 is a fatty acid that has a strong relationship with cognitive function as well as mental health. Fatty fish such as trout, salmon, herring, mackerel and sardines are high in Omega-3. Omega-3-rich foods contain alpha-linolenic acid (ALA) which provides two essential fatty acids: eicosapentaenoic acid (EPA), and docosahexaenoic acid (DHA). EPA and DHA regulate neurotransmitters, reduce inflammation, and promote healthy brain function.

Additionally, sardines and salmons are also rich in Vitamin D.

3.   Vitamin D
          Increasingly vitamin D deficiency is being linked to mood disorders, such as Depression and Anxiety. Studies on pregnant women and older adults have also highlighted how vitamin D help improve mood. Vitamin D may also improve seasonal disaffected disorder (SAD) during winter. Good sources of Vitamin D include cod liver oil, mushrooms, egg yolks, canned tuna, oysters and shrimp. And now many foods are fortified with Vitamin D such as milk, cereal, soy milk and orange juice.

4.   Eggs
          As mentioned above eggs are an excellent source of Vitamin D, but it's also a great source of protein and amino acids. One of the most important amino acids in eggs is tryptophan. It is an amino acid that helps create serotonin. Serotonin is the chemical neurotransmitter that helps regulate mood, sleep, memory, and behavior. Serotonin also improves brain function and relieve anxiety.

5.   Pumpkin Seeds
          Pumpkin seeds are an excellent source of potassium and zinc. Potassium regulates bloods pressure and electrolyte balance. Eating potassium rich foods also help reduce the symptoms of Anxiety and stress. Additionally, zinc is essential for brain and nerve development. The largest zinc deposits in the body are located in the emotion regions of the brain. Zinc deficiency can create emotional difficulties.

6.   Dark Chocolate

Dark chocolate and cocoa in general, has long been thought to improve one's mood. Studies have found lots of evidence to support those assumptions. Chocolate has a high tryptophan content, the mood-enhancing amino acid that helps create good mood chemicals like serotonin.   It is a rich source of polyphenols, especially flavonoids. Studies suggest that flavonoids might reduce neuroinflammation and cell death in the brain. While also improving blood flow. Dark chocolate is also a good source of magnesium which can reduce the symptoms of depression.

7.   Turmeric
Turmeric is a spice normally used in cooking, especially East Asian and Indian cooking. Turmeric's active ingredient curcumin is found to reduce inflammation thereby lowering symptoms of anxiety and lowering oxidative stress that often increase in those suffering from mood disorders. Turmeric was also found to increase DHA.

8.   Chamomile
      Used around the world as an herbal remedy, Chamomile has been hailed for its anti-inflammatory, relaxant, antioxidant, antibacterial properties. Studies have found that while chamomile does not prevent new episodes, it can ease symptoms of anxiety.

9.   Yogurt
      Yogurt contains bifidobacterial and lactobacillus bacteria that have positive effects on brain health. Yogurt and other dairy products can also reduce inflammation in the body. As with other fermented foods like cheese, sauerkraut and kimchi, yogurt increases gut health and reduces anxiety and stress.

10.   Green Tea

    Green tea has become a popular staple of health circles. It contains the amino acid theanine which has anti-anxiety and calming effects. It may also increase the production of serotonin and dopamine in the brain.

    Remember…

    Eating a balanced, high quality, nutrient-dense diet can help ease anxiety.
    Target whole foods with fruit. Legumes, whole grains and lean meats especially fish.
    Include in your diet other foods containing tryptone such as turkey, pineapple, bananas, oats and tofu.
    Since Vitamin E deficiency is linked to mood disorders include nuts especially almonds which are rich the nutrient
    Chia seeds are a good source of Omega-3
    Cinnamon has anti-inflammatory properties
    Spinach and Swiss chard are high in anxiety easing magnesium

 Reducing foods that are high in trans fats, salt, and added sugars can help reduce inflammation in the body.

Managing Anxiety with Therapy

Managing negative thoughts, fears, worries and anxieties can seem like a heavy task. Therapy can help….

Suffering with obsessive thoughts, panic attacks, deep worries or incapacitating phobias can make life seem unbearable, but it's important to know that you don't have to live with anxiety and fear. Therapy is a vital and often the most effective treatment option. Therapy for Anxiety unlike anxiety medication, treats more than just symptoms of the problems. It can help you uncover the underlying causes of the fears and worries that trouble you; teach you relaxation techniques; help you to create a different perspective and re-imagine your life in new and less frightening ways. Therapy can also help you develop more effective coping and problem-solving skills; giving you the tools you need to overcome your anxiety.

Anxiety Disorders vary considerably, so your therapy should be specifically tailored to both your diagnosis and your symptoms. For example, someone who suffers with panic disorder would need very different treatment from someone with obsessive-compulsive disorder (OCD). Length and content of therapy would vary quite a bit. However, Anxiety disorder therapies are generally short-term. The American Psychology Association sites that many improve significantly in 8 to 10 therapy sessions.

Though the diversity of available therapies for anxiety is considerable, the leading approaches are Cognitive Behavioral Therapy (CBT) and Exposure Therapy. Anxiety therapy can be used alone or in conjunction with other types of therapy. These therapies can be conducted in a group setting with those who experience similar anxiety problems or in a more private individual setting. Whichever the setting the goal is the same, to diminish levels of anxiety, calm the mind and conquer your fears.

Cognitive Behavior Therapy

Cognitive Behavior Therapy is defined as a type of psychotherapy in which negative patterns of thought about the self and the world are challenged in order to alter unwanted behavior patterns or treat mood disorders such as depression. (Oxford 2019)

It is the most widely utilized therapy treatment for Anxiety Disorders. Studies have shown it to be effective in the treatment of general anxiety general disorder, panic disorders, social anxiety disorder, phobias and many other conditions.

Cognitive therapy address *cognition*, how we think or process information. Examining how negative thoughts contribute to anxiety. Behavior therapy addresses *behavior* or how we act. How we respond to triggers and other stimuli. Together Cognitive Behavior Therapy (CBT) examines how we process the world and respond to it.

CBT functions from the premise that our thoughts, not external events, effect how we feel and consequently function. In other words, it's not the situation you're in that is fueling your anxiety, but rather your perception of that situation. Consider, for example, you're requested into your boss' office. Consider three different ways you could think about the invitation and how your response to that situation would affect your emotions. It's clear that that situation could provoke different emotions in different individuals; as it could possibly provoke different emotions in your mind alone.

CBT assumes that a singular event can have very different effects on individuals based on their personal attitudes, beliefs, and individual expectations. Those suffering with anxiety disorders have negative ways of thinking that motivate fears and fuel negative emotions. Cognitive Behavior Therapy seeks to identify and correct those destructive views and beliefs. The goal being that, if you change how you think you can in turn change how you feel.

Thought Challenging in CBT for Anxiety

Thought Challenge is the process of challenging the negative thinking patterns that contribute to your anxiety by looking at them from different perspectives instead of automatically assuming them to be facts or truth. Then replacing those negative thoughts with more positive, realistic thought. This process is known as *cognitive reconstructing*.

Thought Challenging has a three-step process:

1.   Identify Your Negative Thoughts
2.   Challenge Those Thoughts
3.   Replace Negative Thoughts with Realistic Thoughts

Step One: Identifying Your Negative Thoughts

With anxiety disorders, situations seem much more threatening than they actually are. For example, to someone suffering with germaphobia, shaking another person's hand can feel like a life- threatening event. To an observer outside of this context, it may seem like an easily identified irrational fear. But within anxiety, identifying fears can be very difficult. One strategy that can help as you try to identify them, is to ask yourself what specifically you were thinking about when you started to feel anxious. Your counselor will help in this process.

Step Two: Challenging Negative Thoughts

In this step the counselor takes the lead. He/she will teach you how to evaluate your anxiety provoking thoughts. Together, you will examine the evidence for your frightening thoughts; analyze adverse beliefs, then finally test the reality of negative predictions. Strategies for challenging negative thoughts will include conducting experiments or tests, weighing the pros and cons of worrying about or avoiding the thing you fear, then determining the realistic probability of actually experiencing the thing that you've been anxious about.

Step Three: Replacing Negative Thoughts with Realistic Thoughts

After you've identified the negative distortions and irrational predictions of anxious thoughts, you can now begin the process of replacing them with new, more positive, more accurate thoughts. With your counselor's help you can formulate realistic, calming statements that you can repeat to yourself when faced with circumstances that would normally cause your anxiety levels to escalate.

Replacing negative thoughts with more realistic ones can be difficult. Many times, negative thinking is the product of life-long patterns of thinking. It takes time to develop a habit. It also takes time and practice to break that habit. That's why Cognitive Behavioral Therapy includes exercises to practice outside of therapy on your own time. Exercises such as:

a. **Feeling the Moment**: Paying Attention to when you feel anxious and not only hearing the thought but recognizing what your body feels like in that moment.

b. **Coping Skills**: Learning coping skills and relaxation techniques to counter anxiety and panic

c. **Confronting Your Fears**: Facing your fears either in your imagination or in real life

Exposure Therapy for Anxiety

Anxiety is filled with cycles of unpleasant and what can feel like uncontrollable sensations. It's natural to try and avoid these feelings. One of the most common ways to avoid anxious feelings is to completely avoid situations that may make you feel anxious. For example, a person with a fear of heights would drive many miles out of their way to avoid a suspension bridge or an overpass. Or someone with fear of public speaking would rather miss a close friend's wedding than give a public toast on their special day. Avoiding fears causes numerous inconveniences and it prevents you from ever having an opportunity to overcome them. In contrast, avoiding fears often makes them more intense.

Exposure Therapy reveals the objects and circumstances that create anxiety. Through repeated sessions, you would face that which causes anxiety. This exposure would increase a feeling of control over the situation, thus diminishing your anxiety. Your counselor will help you to either imagine a menacing situation and confront it or confront a scenario in real life.

Exposure Therapy may be the sole method of therapy or conducted as a part of Cognitive Behavioral Therapy.

Systematic Desensitization

Facing your most intense anxiety right away can be traumatizing, so Exposure Therapy begins with milder, less threatening situations and advances from there. This incremental approach is *systematic desensitization*. Systematic Desensitization allows you to gradually contest fears, develop and build confidence, and master skills to control panic.

Systematic Desensitization involves three steps:

a.   **Relaxation Skills**: The initial step in systematic desensitization is learning techniques. Your counselor will teach such techniques as progressive muscle relaxation or deep breathing. You will practice the technique in therapy and in your own home. Confronting your fears can be jolting. Using the relaxation technique will help you reduce the physical anxiety response in your body and encourage relaxation. Issues such as trembling, and hyperventilation can be mitigated by these techniques.

b.   **Creating a List of Steps**: The second step is to create a list of 10 or more frightening scenarios that you can conquer to reach your goal of overcoming anxiety triggers. If, for example you have a fear of flying, you may begin systematic desensitization by looking at photos of planes in flight and end by taking an actual flight. Each step should be clear and specific; with a precise, measurable objective.

c.   **Working the list**: The final step is to work through your list of fears. The goal is to stay in each identified scenario until those fears subside. This process will teach you that the feelings themselves won't hurt you and that they do go away. In conjunction with your counselor, you will face each fear. Every time the anxiety gets too intense, you will switch to a relaxation technique to help assuage the troubling feelings associated with that situation. Once relaxed, you will return to that situation. These steps will help you to work through each listed scenario without feeling overwhelmed or overly stressed.

Complementary Therapies for Anxiety Disorders

As you examine your Anxiety Disorder in therapy, it may be wise to experiment with complementary therapies designed to bring down your overall levels of distress and help you achieve more emotional balance.

Relaxation Techniques: Techniques like progressive muscle relaxation and mindfulness meditation, when practiced consistently, can reduce anxiety and feelings of emotional health.

Exercise: It's well established that exercise is a natural stress reliever and anxiety reducer. Studies show that at least 30 minutes of exercise three to five times a week can provide a great deal of anxiety relief. For maximum benefit, you should aim for at least an hour of aerobic exercise at least 5 times per week.

Biofeedback: Biofeedback uses sensors to measure precise physiological functions, such as heart rate, muscle tension and breathing. Tracking these and other sensation can teach you to recognize your body's anxiety responses, thereby helping you to learn to control them through relaxation techniques.

Hypnosis: In therapy hypnosis is generally a state of highly focused attention or concentration associated with deep relaxation and intensified suggestibility. It's sometimes used with CBT for treatment of Anxiety. The deep state of relaxation afforded by hypnosis helps you face fears in unique ways.

Making Anxiety Therapy Work for You

Overcoming an Anxiety Disorder takes persistence and time. There are no short cuts. Therapy that involves facing your fears, often means that you will feel worse before you feel better. Avoiding that anxiety may feel better in the short term but the opportunity to overcome that fear will never arise. Commitment to treatment and willingness to follow your counselor's advice is vital. Don't be discouraged by the pace of recovery. Therapy for anxiety is very effective in the long run.

Support your Anxiety therapy by making good choices. Every decision you make from your social life to your personal activity levels affect anxiety. Be intentional in setting yourself up for success by making decisions to encourage relaxation, vitality and a positive mental attitude in your life every day.

Learn About Anxiety. Do your homework. Overcoming anxiety requires that you first understand what it is and how it affects you. While education is not a cure all, it will help you get the most out of therapy.

Strengthen Connections with Others. Anxiety is often birthed out of isolation and loneliness. Connecting with others can help defeat this vulnerability. Purposefully reach out to friends, join a support room and/or connect with a trusted loved one to share your concerns and worries.

Adopt a Healthy Lifestyle. Anxiety not only affects the mind it affects the body. Physical tension and anxiety can be alleviated by regular exercise.

Additionally, avoid alcohol and drugs to cope with any symptoms. Also avoid stimulants like caffeine and nicotine, which make anxiety worse.

Reduce Your Everyday Stress. Scan your life for stress. Once you find it, do what you can to minimize it. Avoid people who make you anxious. Learn to say No. Don't take on extra responsibilities and make time to relax and enjoy your daily life.

DEPRESSION

Depression is a common, universal condition that is characterized by insistently 'depressed' mood that causes a persistent feeling of sadness and loss of interest in activities, significantly impairing daily life.

Depression affects how you think and behave and can lead to a variety of emotional and physical problems. When depressed, one may have trouble doing normal day-to-day activities. Depression symptoms can vary from mild to severe and can lead to a range of behavioral and physical symptoms. More than just a "bout of the blues", Depression isn't a weakness and one can't simply "snap out" of it. Depression can also contribute to a feeling that life isn't worth living and has been associated with thoughts of suicide. Depression may require long-term treatment.

Physical effects of Depression include headaches and light headedness, muscle and joint pain, chest pain and GI issues such as nausea, diarrhea and constipation. Depression is also associated with sleeping too much, sleep difficulties such as insomnia and early wakefulness as well as feelings of exhaustion and fatigue. Depression can also trigger weight gain, weight loss and general eating disorders.

Psychological effects of Depression include sadness; trouble concentrating, remembering details, and making decisions; feelings of guilt, worthlessness, and helplessness; pessimism and hopelessness; irritability, loss of interest in things once pleasurable, including sex; persistent anxious, or "empty" feelings

For Spiritual Support:

My tears have been my meat day and night, while they continually say unto me, Where is thy God?
When I remember these things, I pour out my soul in me: for I had gone with the multitude, I went with them to the house of God, with the voice of joy and praise, with a multitude that kept holy day.
Why art thou cast down, O my soul? And why art thou disquieted in me? Hope thou in God: for I shall yet praise Him for the help of His countenance.
Psalm 42:3-5

The Lord is nigh unto them that are of a broken heart; and saveth such as be of a contrite spirit.
Many are the afflictions of the righteous: but the Lord delivereth him out of them all.
Psalm 34:18-19

Lord, how are they increased that trouble me! Many are they that rise up against me.
Many there be which say of my soul, There is no help for him in God. Selah.
But thou, O Lord, art a shield for me; my glory, and the lifter up of mine head.
Psalm 3:1-3

Depression and Anxiety: Exercise Can Help

Tips to Help You Get Going and Stay Motivated

When you're suffering from depression or anxiety, exercise is often the last thing you'd like to do. However, once you're motivated, exercise can make a considerable difference.

Exercise is vital to health and well-being. It prevents and improves countless health issues including heart disease, high blood pressure and diabetes. Studies show that exercise also has significant effects on psychological well-being; especially depression, anxiety and other mood disorders.

We know for sure that working out and other forms of physical activity eases the symptoms of both depression and anxiety and makes you feel better. Physical activity is now also believed to prevent symptoms from returning once you feel better. In short, with consistency, the chain reactions created in your physical and mental health can improve greatly with increased exercise.

How does exercise help?

Consistent Exercise can help ease depression anxiety by:

Releasing Endorphins into the brain. The chemicals, endogenous cannabinoids, a natural cannabis-like brain chemical and other similar natural brain chemicals are released, enhancing your sense of well-being.

Positive Distraction. The very act of exercising takes the mind off its troubles and diverts thoughts from the unpleasant or worrying cycles that feed depression and anxiety.

Exercise also has many psychological and emotional benefits. It promotes:

Self Confidence. Getting in shape makes you feel good about your appearance. Even early in a fitness journey the very act of meeting exercise goals or challenges great or small boosts self-confidence and makes you feel better.

Broaden Social Interaction. Physical activity increases your chances of meeting and socializing with others. You don't have to be a gym rat to benefit socially from exercise. Simply walking around your neighborhood increases the likelihood that you'll interact with someone and exchange something as simple as a friendly smile which could improve your mood.

Exercise promotes Healthy Coping.

Often avoidance is the preferred coping strategy employed by those suffering with depression or anxiety. There are still others who choose to dwell on negative feelings or simply hope that the feelings dissipate on their own. The introduction of alcohol or drugs can also be a part of that unhealthy coping method. Exercise, on the other hand, provides a positive coping method. It engages the body and the mind with positive results.

Is Structured Exercise the only way?

A structured exercise program definitely yields positive results, but research shows that formal exercise programs are not the only option. Most consistent activity such as regular walking may also help improve your mood. Physical activity and exercise are not exactly the same, but both are beneficial to your health.

Physical activity is any activity that requires energy and engages your muscles. It can include household duties, work or leisure activities.

Exercise is planned, structured activities that include repetitive muscle movement. Unlike physical activity where fitness is a secondary byproduct of that activity, the goal of exercise is to maintain or improve physical fitness.

Exercise is comprised of a wide range of activities designed to boost energy levels, increase physical conditioning and help you feel better. This may conjure visions of running laps around a gym, but exercise can include a number of challenging endeavors.

Certainly, exercises like weight training, rowing, running and other fitness activities that get the heart pumping will be beneficial. But, physical activities like washing your car, gardening or even taking a walk around the block can also boost your mood. Activities like these get you off the couch, out of your house and often out of your head.

If you're not a fitness buff, increasing your exercise or physical activity can seem daunting, but it may not be as difficult as you think. A broader view of physical activity can include finding ways to add small amounts of activity throughout your day. You don't have to do it all at once. Take the stairs instead of the elevator. Park a little farther from an entrance and you've just fit in a short walk. Live near your job or the local grocery store, consider a ride instead of driving.

How Much Is Enough?

The standard for effective exercise is 30 minutes a day for three to five days a week. This standard can significantly improve the symptoms of depression and anxiety. But smaller amounts of physical activity, as little as 10 to 15 minutes at a time, may also make a difference. Engaging in vigorous activities such as running, or bicycling can improve your mood in a much shorter period of time.

The long-term mental health benefits of physical activity and exercise may be contingent upon your consistency. Finding an activity you enjoy will help you stick with it.

Get Started and Get Motivated

Starting an exercise routine can be exciting but sticking with it can be more of a challenge. Taking these steps can help.

Find Something You Like. Exercise won't be successful if you hate doing it. Its important that you figure out what activity you like to do and what you would consistently follow through with. For example, would you be more likely to bike to work, take an early morning jog or play ball with your kids after school? Decide what you enjoy and stay with it.

Get Support from a Counselor. Talk to your counselor or mental health professional for guidance and support. Discuss your treatment plan and which exercise or physical activity plan would best fit in it.

Set Sensible Goals. Don't overwhelm yourself with exercise goals. Your mission doesn't have to be jogging an hour a day five days a week. Be realistic about your capacity and begin gradually. Customize your plan to your needs and abilities and stay away from goals you're unlikely to meet.

Be positive. Don't turn your exercise routine into a chore. If it becomes another "should" then it's likely you won't be consistent. Schedule your exercise activities the same as you would therapy sessions or medication. Treat it as one of the tools to help you get better. And stay positive about the great results you can look forward to.

Analyze Your Barriers. Take stock of what barriers may be stopping you from being physically active. Then find solutions. For example, if you're self- conscious a solution could be to exercise at home. If you follow through better with a comrade, ask a friend to be your work out buddy. If money is a barrier, exercise in the park and skip the expensive gear. Make being physically active a priority and work through barriers.

Give Yourself Credit. Give yourself credit for every step you take in the right direction. Even the smallest move forward is a move forward. Be prepared for setbacks and obstacles. Life happens, just don't quit. Missing one day of your routine doesn't mean that all is lost. It just means that you must try again the next day.

Should I see my doctor?

You should consult a physician before beginning any new exercise program. That way, you'll know for sure that it will be both safe and effective. Discuss the activities you're considering and find out if that intensity level is appropriate for you. Discuss any medications you may be taking and any health conditions you may have and possible side effects. Your doctor can provide you with helpful advice about how to get started and how to stay motivated.

Exercise and physical activity can provide an ideal boost to your mental health. It can ease symptoms and help you manage anxiety and depression. However, if you exercise regularly and depression and anxiety still interfere with your daily life, see your doctor or mental health provider. Remember though exercise and physical activity are great for easing symptoms they are not a substitute for therapy or medication.

Depression Treatment

Therapy, Medication, Self Help. If you're unsure which treatment option for depression is best for you, here's how you decide.

Deciphering your depression treatment options

When you're suffering with depression, it can feel like you're living under a dark cloud that you can't escape. But rest assured, even the most severe depression can be treated. If depression is hindering your ability to live a satisfying life, don't hesitate to seek help. From therapy to medication to lifestyle changes, there are several different, effective options available to you.

No two people are affected by depression in the same way. So, reasonably that there's no "one size fits all" cure for it. What could bring relief for one, may not work at all for someone else. To find the most effective treatment for you, it's vital that you be as informed as possible. Matching with the appropriate treatment could help you overcome depression and reclaim your life.

Tips on Depression Treatment

Learn as much as you can. Together with your health care provider, learn as much about your specific depression diagnosis. Learn what is the severity of your symptoms. Severe depression requires more intensive treatment. Also, find out whether your depression is in any way connected to another underlying illness or condition that may require treatment. Treating that condition in addition to your depression is vital successfully alleviating your symptoms and experiencing long-term relief.

Take Your Time Finding the Right Treatment. Be patient as you attempt to find the treatment that works for you. It may take a bit of trial and error to find the fit that's right for you. For example, if you decide to pursue therapy as a primary method of treatment, your first therapist may not be the best fit for you. Or you may find that exercise works better than your newly prescribed medication. Be open to change and take however much deliberation you may need.

Don't rely on medication alone. Certainly, medication has been proven effective in the treatment of depression symptoms, however it is not usually suitable for long-term use. Treatments such as therapy and exercise can be as effective as medication, without the unwanted side effects. In some cases, these treatments may work better. Find the fit that best works for you.

Cultivate Social Support. Social connections are a great resource to protect you from depression. When you're feeling stuck, having a trusted family member or friend to reach out to can be invaluable. Or cultivating connections within a depression support group can also be a source of strength. Utilizing your support systems is not a sign of weakness. It takes enormous strength to ask for help especially when really a face to face conversation could really help.

Remember that Treatment Takes Time and Commitment. All depression treatments take time, so you must commit to the process. That process may seem slow or overwhelming, but take heart, this is normal. Recovery is filled with ebbs and flows, but eventually stability comes.

Lifestyle Change: An essential part of treatment

Lifestyle changes are a powerful tool in the treatment of depression. Sometimes these changes can be all that you need. Even if other treatment is needed, lifestyle changes can help you lift the fog of depression faster.

Lifestyle changes that benefit depression treatment

Exercise. In some cases, consistent exercise can be as effective in treating depression as medication. Exercise boosts serotonin, endorphins and other feel good chemicals in your brain. It also triggers the growth of new brain cells and connections, much like antidepressants. Most of all you don't have to run a 5k to reap the benefits. 30 minutes a day for 3 to 5 days can make a tremendous difference. For maximum results shoot for 60 minutes of aerobic exercise on most days.

Social Support. Strong social connections are a key factor in relieving depression. Isolation can exacerbate the effects of depression. Stay in contact with friends and family. Consider joining a group or taking a class. Volunteering is also a wonderful way to help yourself as you help others.

Nutritional Support. Good nutrition is important for both physical and mental health. Eating small, balanced meals throughout the day will keep your blood sugar levels stable, which minimizes mood swings and gives you steady flow of energy all day. While sugary foods may provide a quick boost, they also cause a "sugar crash". Complex carbohydrates are a much better nutritional choice.

Sleep. Studies have shown that sleep has strong effects on mood. Sleep deprivation can worsen your depression symptoms. It causes irritability, moodiness and sadness. Be sure to get enough sleep every night. It's recommended that you get at least 7 hours of sleep a night. Between 7 and 9 hours are optimal.

Reduce Stress. High levels of stress can worsen depression. Be intentional in your efforts to reduce stress levels. Make lifestyle changes to reduce stress where possible and manage it when not. Resist stressors like work overload and unsupportive relationships or find ways to minimize their impact.

Ruling Out Illness as the Source of Depression

Depression can have many causes. One that elude detection is physical illness. If you're depressed and lifestyle changes haven't caused any improvement you should see your physician for a thorough check-up. Depression caused by physical illness won't be affected in any meaningful way by therapy or medication. The underlying medical issue must be addressed first. Allow your doctor to assess for medical conditions that can mimic depression. And be sure to report all medications you are taking, as your depression may be a drug induced side effect.

There are many conditions and medications that can cause symptoms of depression such as fatigue, sadness and feeling a loss of enjoyment. Hypothyroidism is one such illness. This underactive thyroid disease is a common mood disrupter, especially in women. Those on several daily medications are also at high risk for depression-like symptoms. The higher the number of medications you take the greater the risk of drug interactions. Be sure to work closely with your doctor to lessen the risk of these potential issues.

Psychotherapy Treatment for Depression

Once its determined that there no underlying medical causes for your depression, then Psychotherapy or talk therapy can be an extremely effective treatment. With talk therapy, you can gain insight in to the underlying mental and emotional causes of your depression. From there, you can learn the skills needed cope and prevent the depression from coming back.

The three main types of talk therapy are cognitive behavior therapy, interpersonal therapy and psycho-dynamic therapy. They can be used separately or in a blended approach.

In psychotherapy you can learn many techniques including how to reframe negative thinking and how to use behavioral skills to combat depression. Therapy can help you get to the root of your depression and really work through it. It can give the skills to understand why you harbor certain feelings as well as identify your triggers. Therapy can help you see what you need to do to get healthy and stay that way.

Seeing the Big Picture in Therapy

With depression, one often feels overwhelmed and has difficulty focusing. Therapy can help you center yourself and see the totality of the situation and realize what may be contributing to your depression and make changes. There are specific areas that this approach can help with:

Handling your problems. Your counselor can help you talk through situations and provide positive feedback. Then you can discover more constructive ways to handle life's challenges.

Setting Healthy Boundaries. The inability to say "No" is often a source of stress, especially for those suffering with depression. The lack of appropriate boundaries in relationships and at work can make you feel overwhelmed and sad. Therapy can help you see your limitations and create boundaries that are right for you.

Relationships. Therapy can help you identify your relationship patterns and build more healthy ones. Better relationships will reduce the isolation that exacerbates depression. This type of therapy will also help improve current relationships and build social support.

Individual or Group Therapy: Which do you choose?

The view of "real therapy" is usually that of one-on-one private sessions with a counselor. However, a group setting can be extremely effective as well. The key is finding the situation that is best for you. Therapy for depression can be done effectively in either a private setting or a group setting. They are similarly held for about an hour and are designed to provide maximum support and information to help develop skills to overcome depression.

In individual therapy, you can build a strong rapport with your counselor in a private setting. You may feel more comfortable sharing sensitive information in this environment. You also get individualized attention and learn skills focused only on you and your experiences.

In group therapy, the setting is still a confidential setting, but it includes peers with similar experiences. Group therapy allows group members to see similar emotional occurrences from different points of view. It would include people who have been "in the trenches" and are also working through challenges. Often group members inspire one another and share ideas and provide each other social support. Group settings also combat the social isolation that plagues those suffering with depression and offers a much-needed network.

When Therapy Gets Tough

In the natural course of therapy things will get difficult. Facing issues with depression painful experiences arise. The temptation to give up can rear its head, but don't. Resist the temptation to retreat into self-defeating habits. Instead, discuss your feelings openly and honestly with your counselor and work through your challenges. In those times, having a strong trusting relationship with your counselor is very important.

However, if the connection with your counselor consistently starts to feel uncomfortable, don't be afraid to explore other therapeutic options. Trust is the foundation of effective therapy.

Finding A Therapist

Choosing a mental healthcare provider is a very important decisions to consider. In choosing a counselor, remember that you're looking for an informed, compassionate, supportive partner in treatment and recovery. There are many ways to find a counselor:

Your primary care physician. Consult your doctor. He can make a referral for a good counselor.

National Mental Associations. Providers can be found on the websites of national mental health providers or you can contact them by phone

Word of mouth. Family or friends may know a good provider they trust.

Community Organizations. Community mental health clinics, churches or senior centers offer mental health services on a sliding scale and may able to refer you to other services.

Medication for Depression

Treatment for depression is a very individualized process. One of the most popular treatments for depression is medication or antidepressants. But, just because it's the most popular doesn't mean it most effective. Medication can help some relieve the symptoms of some moderate to severe depression symptoms. However, since depression is not solely about a chemical imbalance in the brain, it does little to cure the underlying problems causing the depression.

Antidepressants also have side effects and safety concerns. So, if you're considering antidepressant medication, remember that it is not a long-term solution and should be paired with other treatments.

Is medication from your primary doctor a good idea?

If you're depressed, your primary care physician will probably be the first person to recognize it. In most cases, when you're not well your primary doctor prescribes something to help you heal. However, in this case that may not be the best option. Instead, allow your doctor to give you a referral. You should explore any mental health issues with a physician who specializes in mental health treatment. They may find that you don't need medication at all. And if you do, they would be best suited to advise you on your options.

Transcranial Magnetic Stimulation (TMS)

Some symptoms of depression can be resistant to therapy, medication and lifestyle changes or self-help. There is still help. Transcranial Magnetic Stimulation (TMS) is an option. TMS is a noninvasive treatment that directs magnetic electric pulses into the regions of the brain that control mood. These pulses can stimulate brain cells which improve communication between parts of the brain and ease depression symptoms.

TMS can improve symptoms for treatment resistant depression. It can improve energy and drive. This uptick in well-being can enable you to begin talk therapy or lifestyle changes, like exercise and improving diet. However, it's not a cure-all. Like medication it's a short-term fix and should be done under the supervision of your therapist.

Alternative and Complimentary Treatments

There are some nonconventional treatments for depression including vitamins, herbal supplements, acupuncture and relaxation techniques. These treatments are not necessarily curing, but they can have positive effects.

Vitamins and supplements
Some depression can be caused by nutritional deficiency. In those cases, vitamins and supplements can help. Even though most supplements and vitamins are deemed safe for over the counter use, it's still best that any attempts to treat symptoms of depression be done under the guise of your doctor. And natural and herbal supplements can have side effects, as well as drug and food interactions.

Relaxation Techniques

Relaxation can reduce symptoms of depression, reduce stress and boost feelings of well-being. Yoga, deep breathing, meditation and progressive muscle relaxation are all great ways to treat your symptoms. And best of all, they're side effect free.

Acupuncture

Acupuncture is a holistic complementary medical practice that entails penetrating the skin with fine needles to stimulate specific points on the body. It's been known to help with various conditions including depression. If you choose acupuncture to compliment your depression treatment, be certain to utilize a licensed qualified professional.

Depression

The Effects on your Body

Depression is a mental health disorder that effects millions of people. However, it also effects your total physical health and well-being. Depression symptoms can surface in ways that you expect and in ways that may seem unrelated. Left untreated depression can really harm your body. Here are some of the common effects:

Brain:
o   Trouble with Memory
o   Insomnia
o   Feelings of sadness
o   Preoccupation with death

Heart:
o   Risk of heart attack
o   Feelings of clinginess

Digestive System:
o Weight Gain
o Weight Loss
o Poor Digestion

Circulatory System:
o Constricted Blood Vessels
o Fatigue

Nervous System:
o   Increased Sensitivity to Pain
o   Weakened Immune system

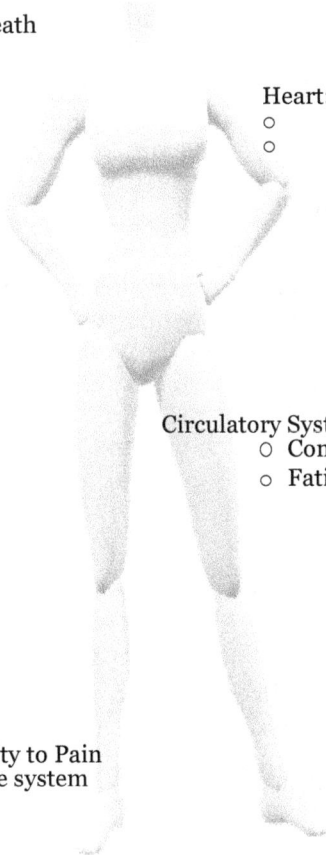

Feeling sad or nervous sometimes is a normal life, but when these feelings become persistent and uncontrollable, they could be symptoms of Depression. Left untreated depression can have residual effects that harm both your mental and physical health.

Central Nervous System

Depression can do a lot of damage to the central nervous system. It can manifest itself as memory loss, loss in reaction time and difficulty putting feelings into words. You may also feel tired all the time or have trouble sleeping. Experiencing irritability and anger may also manifest as well as loss of interest in sex.

People who are depressed often have trouble concentrating and making decisions. It can also cause problems with neurological illness like epilepsy, Alzheimer's disease and multiple sclerosis.

Children with depression may be harder to diagnose because they don't articulate their feelings as fluidly as adults, but they can also display excessive irritability, persistent worry and clinginess that don't resolve over time.

Digestive System

Though depression is a mental illness can have an immense effect on your digestive system. Obvious symptoms like binge overeating or severe loss of appetite can lead to issues of obesity and weight related illness; and anorexia and other nutrient deficiency problems. However, depression can also cause digestive issues like stomach cramps, constipation and severe malnutrition. Lifestyle changes that include eating nutritious, consistent meals are vital to mental health.

Cardiovascular and Immune systems

Cardiovascular problems like high blood pressure, high cholesterol and heart disease are connected to depression. Inflammation is also associated with depression. Inflammation causes many diseases in the body. Prominent risk of heart attack is common with depression.

ANGER MANAGEMENT

Anger is a strong feeling of annoyance, hostility and/or displeasure. It is an emotion characterized by antagonism toward someone or something one feels deliberately wronged by. Anger can present opportunities to express negative feelings and motivate to find solutions to problems.

Anger as an emotional state is experienced by everyone and occurs in various forms and degrees of intensity. However, excessive as well as misplaced Anger can cause problems to both the mental and physical health.

Anger Management is the process of learning to recognize signs that you're becoming angry and to calm down; to deal with situations in appropriately productive ways. Anger Management does not try to prevent feelings of Anger or encourage the repression of them. It simply gives the tools necessary to recognize frustrations early and resolve them in a way that allows for the expression of needs while calm and in control.

Physical effects of excessive Anger include headaches, increased blood pressure, increased heart rate, restlessness, muscles tension, tingling, heart palpitations or tightening of the chest, pressure in the head or sinus cavities, eczema, fatigue, hormonal imbalance and depressed immune system. These effects can lead to serious long-term health problems including chronic high blood pressure, reduced lung function, heart attack, stroke, chronic infections and even cancer.

Psychological effects of excessive Anger include low self-esteem, depression, rage, mood disturbances, anxiety, guilt, general hostility, feelings of dejection, mental fatigue, confusion, frustration, aggravation and resentment.

For Spiritual Support:

Wherefore, my beloved brethren, let every man be swift to hear, slow to speak, slow to wrath:
For the wrath of man worketh not the righteousness of God.
James 1:19-20

Be ye angry, and sin not: let not the sun go down upon your wrath Neither give place to the devil.
Let him that stole steal no more: but rather let him labor, working with his hands the thing which is good, that he may have to give to him that needeth.
Let no corrupt communication proceed out of your mouth, but that it may minister grace unto the hearers.
And grieve not the Holy Spirit of God, whereby ye are sealed unto the day of redemption.
Let all bitterness, and wrath and anger and clamor and evil speaking, be put away from you with all malice:
And be ye kind tenderhearted, forgiving one another , even as God for Christ's sake hath forgiven you.
Ephesians 4:26-32

Anger Management:
Tips to Control the Fury

Every one of us has "lost it" at some point. Be it, a traffic jam when you're in a hurry or a blowout at a family function, we all know what it's like to get worked up. Anger doesn't feel good, but when utilized positively, it can motivate you to make changes in things that simply aren't working for you.

But unchecked anger can lead to problems in your mind and body; as well as create chaos in your social life. Your body begins to feel the chemical rush and respond to what should be a temporary state of alert. Simultaneously, you become aggressive, unreasonable, irrational and difficult to be around. The end result is you, sick in your body, isolated and overwrought.

Some are more likely than others to have difficulty controlling their anger. Those under extreme stress may find it more challenging to control anger. Those with traumatic brain injury are likely to experience overwhelming uncontrolled anger. Those with mental health issues, especially children may have difficulty controlling their anger.

Regardless the circumstance, there is help for you. One resource that can help is Anger Management Exercise. They help you to calm down, reduce outbursts and improve overall well-being. If you're struggling with anger use these exercises to help you.

Breathe

When you become angry, your breathing becomes quick and shallow. One way to calm down is to slow your breathing. Breathe slowly through your nose and out of your mouth. Breathe deeply from your belly not your chest. Repeat breaths until you feel yourself calming down.

Progressive Muscle Relaxation

Muscle tension is another sign of stress in the body you may feel when you're angry.
To release the tension in your body, focus on one muscle group at a time. Consider starting at the head and working your way down. Or if you prefer vice versa. Slowly tense the muscle group, hold for a few seconds, then release. Repeat this process until you work through every muscle group in your body.

Visualization

Visualizing yourself relaxed can actually relax you. Use your imagination to see yourself calm. Sit quiet and close your eyes. Imagine a relaxing place. It can be a memory or somewhere new. Allow you mind to flow. Listen for the sights, the sounds, the smells and enjoy your little getaway.

Get Moving

Besides being beneficial for your physical health, exercise is a very effective stress reliever. It calms anger and reduces stress in the body and mind. Try to exercise every day to keep the anger and stress away. During a flare up, take a brisk walk or bike ride. Do something physical and you'll definitely feel better.

Know Your Triggers

Typically, people get angry over the same issues repeatedly. Stop the cycle. Take a moment to really think about what makes you angry. Then make a note of it, mental or physical. Make a real effort to solve the challenge and if not possible, to avoid it.
Instead walking into a trigger blindly, learn to recognize it and take decisive action.

Stop and Listen

In an angry state, it's easy to just to conclusions. You may find yourself saying or doing things that are unkind simply because you've misunderstood. Stop and listen. Consider the entire situation before you react. Or in a discussion, take a moment to try to hear the other person out before responding. Then allow yourself to really think about your answer. If the tension has escalated beyond what you can handle in the moment, simply tell them that you need to step away.

Change Your Mind

Anger can exacerbate your perceptions and make you think situations are much worse than they really are. This in turn feeds more anger. Reduce anger by changing your negative thoughts into realistic ones. Avoid extreme words like "never" and "always" in your thinking and descriptions. Try to adopt a balanced world and turn your demands into requests.

Don't Dwell on Things

Dwelling, rehashing, contemplating, pondering or simply stewing; no matter which term you choose, it's not good to mentally relive something that made you angry over and over.

Dwelling on situations only keep you angry longer. Memory is interesting in that the ability to see things accurately distorts over time. The likelihood of your remembering a situation lessens but your anger over it can grow. Take the positive parts and leave the rest in the past.

Know Your Body

When you're angry, your body experiences a series of reactions. Your heart rate, blood pressure and breathing increases. Your body temperature elevates, and your system is flooded with stress hormones. All these reactions are signals that your body is on high alert. Pay attention to your body. In addition to these signals you may experience something unique, like a slight headache or an eye twitch. When you feel these warning signals take action. Step away from the situation that is upsetting you or use a relaxation technique to help you calm down.

Get Help for Your Anger

Learning to manage your anger is a process. It takes time and happens more quickly for some than others. If your anger is overwhelming or causing you to harm yourself or others, it's time to seek expert help.

Talk to your primary care doctor to get a referral to a trained counselor. This expert will help you find a treatment plan that will work for you. Some treatments include cognitive behavioral therapy, medication and behavior modification techniques.

The bottom line is uncontrolled anger can impact your life in many negative ways, but anger management can give you the tools you need to governor your emotions.

Anger Management:

10 Ways to Keep Yourself in Check

Anger is a very normal and healthy behavior. Everyone loses their temper every now and then. But when you become so angry that you're unable to control, yourself it's time to check your temper.

Uncontrolled anger can cause strains in relationships, trouble in your work environment, and health problems. It's very important to keep deal with your anger in a positive way. Here are 10 tips to help you do it:

1.   Think before you speak: When you're angry, several things are happening in your body and mind. Your adrenaline is flowing, and you are in "fight mode". The heat of the moment is not the best time to have a meaningful conversation, but if you must, Think Before You Speak. The very act of thinking will cause you to slow down and in turn calm down. Remember, words have power. Once it's out there you can't take it back.

2.   Speak When You're Calm: Calm down and let your mind can clear. Any concerns or frustrations expressed before then may be tainted by your angry. If you want to be heard, speak after you've calmed down. You will be able to express your concerns directly and clearly.

3.   Take a Timeout: When you feel yourself becoming irritated or stressed, take a moment. A little quiet can prevent you from blowing up and help you to regroup. Timeouts are not just for kids. They could present a perfect

opportunity to clear your head.

4.   Workout: Exercise is a great way to destress. It can help you utilize some of the energy your anger is generating. When you feel yourself getting angry, take a brisk walk. Or go out and do something physical you enjoy.

5.   Try to Find Resolutions: Don't focus on what's making you angry. Focus on finding solutions. If your kid's always leaving his clothes on the floor, buy him a hamper. If your partner's always late for dinner, try to find a later time that works for both of you. Instead of stewing, remind yourself anger doesn't solve anything.

6.   Use "I" Statements: In expressing yourself, avoid blaming and criticizing. This increases tension, rather than bringing clarity. "I" statements allow you to say what you need to say without pointing a finger. You can be both specific and respectful.

7.   Let It Go: Don't hold grudges. Forgiveness can be a very powerful thing. Negative feelings, like unforgiveness, can crowd out positive feelings. They can turn into bitterness and leave you wallowing in a sense of offense and injustice. Instead of being stuck, let it go. Allow yourself to learn from the situation and move on.

8.   Remember Your Sense of Humor: When possible... laugh. As you face situations that make you angry, instead of feeding your anger find some humor in them. Unrealistic expectations can be hilarious. Lightening up a situation through humor can break tension and help you decompress.

9.   Relaxation Techniques: To control your anger and decrease feelings of destress, put your relaxation skills to work. Practice deep breathing. Listen to music. Exercise. Use calming statements to help refocus you. These methods will benefit your mind and body.

10.   If You Need Help, Get it: Learning to control anger can be difficult. Everyone faces moments they wish they could have handled better. But if your anger is out of your control, get help. There's no reason to feel ashamed and there are many resources that can support you. Or that you may harm yourself or someone else.

.

Anger: Tips to Managing

Anger

It can be a positive and useful emotion to help you make changes you may need

It has physical as well as emotional effects on your body

The physical effects can be long-term and negative

There are effective strategies to help you manage anger including, exercise, relaxation techniques and counseling

Anger is a natural occurring emotion that every human being experiences. It can be helpful and appropriate and in the proper context. When expressed properly, anger can give you the push needed to insightfully make the changes.

Anger is a powerful emotion. Out of control it can have destructive results. It can lead to physical and emotional health issues, physical fights, arguments, abuse and even self-harm.

Physical Effects of Anger

Anger triggers the fight or flight response in the body. There are several emotions triggered in this response including excitement, fear and anxiety. Stress hormones flood the body from the adrenal gland. Adrenaline and cortisol courses through the body. The brain pulls blood from the gut and sends it into the muscles to prepare for physical exertion. The heart rate, respiration and the blood pressure rises; as does the body's temperature. The mind sharpens and focuses on the moment.

Health problems with Anger

Unfortunately, the constant flood of stress chemicals and metabolic changes that occur with unrestrained anger can cause harm to many different systems of the body. Some of those health problems include:

Headaches

Digestion issue

Abdominal pain

Insomnia

Anxiety

Depression

High Blood Pressure

Skin problems like eczema

Heart attack

Stroke

Healthy Ways to Express Anger

Recognize and accept that anger is a normal emotion

If you feel out of control, walk away until you cool off

Try to pinpoint the exactly why you're angry

Once you've found the problem, consider these initial easy strategies to help remedy it:

Talk to some you trust

Do something physical to relieve the inner stress

Unhealthy Ways to Deal with Anger

There are many harmful ways to express anger, including:

Explosive Anger:

Some people have little control over their anger and tend to have explosive anger or rages. Raging anger can lead to physical abuse and violence.

Often people who fly into rages have low self esteem and use their anger as a way to manipulate others and feel powerful. They wreak havoc and then feel guilty and isolate themselves from family and friends.

Anger Repression:

When the person considers anger inappropriate or "bad" they choose to repress it. But bottled anger often turns into depression and anxiety. This causes a host of other emotional problems. Repression then explodes on someone or something innocent such as pets or loved ones.

Dealing with Arguments

During an argument, it's easy to stay angry with the person with whom you're arguing. Not resolving the argument can lead to very uncomfortable situations, especially if you see them often.

Talking to that person about your disagreement, may or may not help. If you choose to approach them try to do it in a productive way. Stay calm and communicate as openly and honestly as you can.

If they can be abusive or violent and you still choose to engage them, a phone call may be a more prudent choice; to see if they are open to resolving the disagreement. If you feel safe doing so, ask someone to be there with you for support both during the call and afterwards.

Tell the person how you feel but avoid telling them how they feel. Remember, it is possible to agree to disagree. If the issue requires a solution between both parties, you may need to have a third party mediate the conflict and help you both see one another's point of view.

Reasons to deal with Arguments:

As a result of working through it, you may develop a healthier relationship.

You may feel more relaxed and healthier. You may even sleep better.

You'll feel happier

.

Managing Anger Long-Term

Changing how you express your anger can take time and effort. Here are some suggestions:

Learn relaxation techniques, like deep breathing

See a counselor if you're harboring anger over issues in your past.

Exercise Regularly!

Exercise and Mood Management

People under stress are more likely to frustration and anger. Studies show that regular exercise works wonders to improve your mood and reduce stress. This is likely attributed to the facts that exercise burns stress chemicals and boosts mood regulating neurotransmitters, like endorphins and catecholamines.

Teaching Children Management Anger

We've discussed how difficult it is for an adult to manage anger. Imagine a frustrated child attempting to manage an emotion as powerful as anger without years of experience or emotional maturity. Here's how you can help your child:

Lead by example.

Treat your child's feelings respectfully.

Encourage open and honest communication at home.

Teach them practical problem solving.

Make sure they know that anger is a natural emotion and okay when expressed appropriately.

Allow them to express their anger appropriately.

Teach your child self-soothing and calming techniques

Have consequences for aggressive or violent behavior but encourage appropriate expressions.

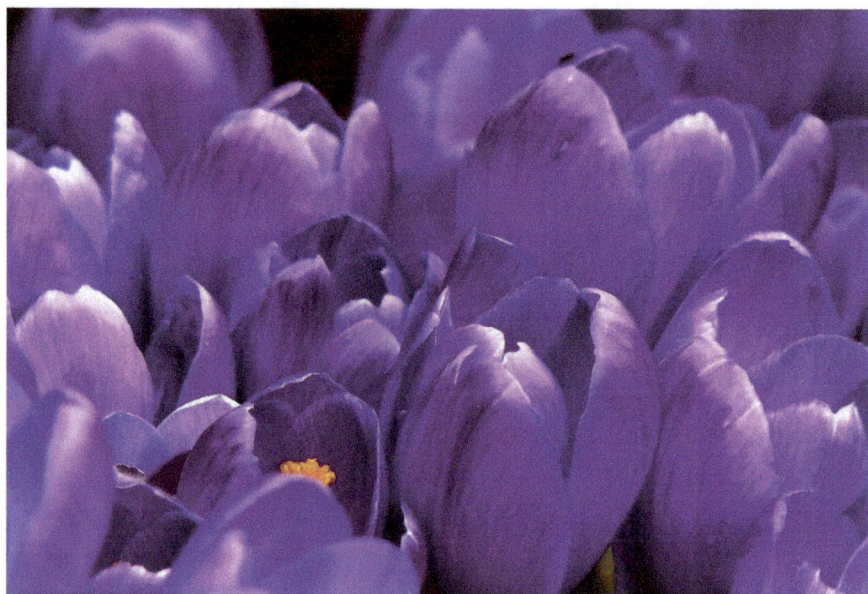

PREMARITAL COUNSELING

Premarital Counseling is therapy that helps couples prepare for marriage by giving tools, information and education to help ensure that both partners understand the institution of marriage, commitment and are striving for a strong, healthy relationship. This counseling gives couples a better chance for a stable and satisfying marriage.

Premarital Counseling is unique to other therapies in that the focus is primarily preventive. In addition to educating, this counseling helps couples identify weaknesses that could become potential problems during marriage. Premarital Counseling allows them the opportunity to give marriage more deliberate consideration. It is also an important tool for assessing the readiness of potential couples.

Premarital Counseling therapy seeks to counter at least seven influences that can contribute to unhealthy marriages including:
Unrealistic expectations
Personal Immaturity
Changing roles in marriage

Commonly accepted alternate forms of marriage
Loosening sexual standards
Previous experience with marriage
Circumstances that can signal high risks for a marriage

Premarital Counseling seeks to help couples prevent marital problems and personal conflicts. It identifies issues that could make married life difficult and unfulfilling. And affords couples the invaluable opportunity to learn from the mistakes of others.

For Spiritual Support:

Whoso findeth a wife findeth a good thing, and obtaineth favor of the Lord.
Proverbs 18:22

But from the beginning of the creation God made them male and female.
For this cause shall a man leave his father and mother, and cleave to his wife;
And they twain shall be one flesh: so then they are no more twain, but one flesh.
What therefore God hath joined together, let not man put asunder.
Mark 10:6-9

Let thy fountain be blessed: and rejoice with the wife of thy youth.
Let her be as the loving hind and pleasant roe; let her breasts satisfy thee at all times; and be thou ravished always with her love.
And why wilt thou, my son, be ravished with a strange woman, and embrace the bosom of a stranger?
Proverbs 5:18-20

MARRIAGE COMPATIBILITY TEST

Marriage is a beautiful institution, filled with a lifetime of laughter and love. But there will be instances that test the breadth of those chuckles and make you wonder "how deep is your love". So, before you say "I do" there may be a few things you and your intended should discuss. You may find that your "I do" has a few "Are you crazies" lurking in the shadows.

Answer each question individually and honestly. There are no right or wrong answers. Compare and discuss your responses with your beloved. And remember it's all in fun!

1. When watching TV, custody of the remote controls belongs to:

    a.   The King of the Castle
    b.   WIFE
    c.   Whoever turned the TV on
    d.   Whoever wins the wrestling match

2.   The toilet seat should be

a. Down, lid closed
b. Down, lid up
c. Up
d. It doesn't really matter
e. Down in her bathroom, Up in his

3.   Entertaining friends for dinner should be

a. A Catered Affair
b. A sit-down meal lovingly prepared in your kitchen
c. Potluck
d. Definitely… Takeout

4.   Dirty clothes belong

a. In the hamper of course
b. As close to the hamper as I have time to put it
c. On the floor in the room near the hamper is fine
d. On the furniture in the room near the hamper, no problem
e. Near the bed so you can wear them again the next day

5.   A new car should be chosen based on
a. Purchase price
b. Performance, repair and insurance costs
c. Color
d. Cup holders and mirrors
e. What the coworkers are driving

6.   In winter, appropriate temperature for a house is

a. 75° or higher
b. about 70°
c. about 60°
d. Breath-cycles

7.   Home-cooked food is best when

        a. Eaten immediately after preparation
        b.Made just like mom used to make it
        c. Ketchup is the main topping
        d. The fire department doesn't have to be involved

8.   The best way to travel on vacation is

        a. By plane
        b. By train
        c. By car
        d. On foot through the wilderness
        e. Separately, to different destinations

9.   Trips to the mall should be made when

        a. You really need something specific
        b. There's a SALE
        c. It's raining and there's nothing else to do
        d. You get a new credit card

10..   The volume on the stereo should be set

        a. Low enough for normal conversation
        b. Low enough to not annoy the neighbors
        c. Loud enough to appreciate the quality of the recording
        d. Loud enough to feel vibrations
        e. Structural Damage

11.   Laundry should be done....

        a. Weekly
        b. Twice a week
        c. Every other week
        d. As soon as you run out of clean underwear

12. My idea of an exotic vacation destination is

  a. Thailand
  b. Mexico
  c. Hawaii
  d. North Dakota

13. Repainting the living room should be done by

  a. A licensed professional
  b. The two of us working in harmony
  c. The college kid down the street
  d. Whoever's idea it was to repaint the room
  e. The time your mother arrives to visit

14. When buying a new TV, it is important to consider

  a. Will it fit your budget
  b. Will it fit through your door
  c. What will fit in the new Entertainment Center you're
     buying with it
  d. How many people will fit in your house to watch the Game

15. Before having children, you should be together for

  a. At least one year
  b. At least two years
  c. At least five years
  d. At least six months
  e. One really romantic evening

16. Eating in bed is....

  a. A No-No, under any circumstances
  b. Okay only if you're really sick
  c. Acceptable if served on a proper bed tray
  d. The best way to enjoy late night TV
  e. A harmless way to avoid sex

17. The best videos to stream are

   a. The absolute newest releases
   b. The Classics all the way
   c. Definitely Romantic Comedies
   d. Action Packed
   e. XXX

18. When you feel you should lose weight, your partner should

   a. Insist that you're perfect just the way you are
   b. Join you in your weight-loss program
   c. Buy you a gym membership
   d. Move out until your diet is over

19. When the wife is upset or angry, the husband should....

   a. Be comforting
   b. Be quiet
   c. Help her solve her problem
   d. Rationally, tell her to get over it
   e. Apologize, since she must believe it's his fault

20. Household chores should be done by....

   a. Wifey
   b. Hubby
   c. Both
   d. The maid
   e. The kids, isn't that why you had them

21. When decorating your first home, the furnishings should be

   a. The latest trends
   b. An eclectic blend of antique and new
   c. Whatever you can afford, even if it's clearance
   d. Whatever you can swipe from your parents' homes

22.   You should attend a place of worship

a. Weekly
b. Monthly
c. On major holidays
d. When your mom's in town
e. When you find one that serves Screaming Eagle Cabernet
    1992

23.   Taking out the garbage is the responsibility of
a. The Man of the House
b. The Lady of the House
c. Whoever put the last item in
d. Whoever's going out anyway

24.   My perfect birthday party is

a. A romantic dinner for two
b. Cake and coffee with our good friends
c. A small gathering with family
d. An impressive surprise party with family and friends
e. A spectacular event that would rival a Presidential inaugural

25.   If we have an argument, we should

a. Kiss and make up before we go to bed
b. Sit down and discuss it like two rational people
c. Go to separate rooms until we cool off
d. Contact a marriage counselor
e. Call a friend who knows God's Word

Know Your Partner Worksheet

<u>Fun and Games</u>

What Music did your partner listen to as a kid?

Where is your partner's dream vacation spot?

What's your partner's favorite present-day TV show?

What upcoming event is your partner looking forward to?

What book that has influenced your partner significantly?

The Future

How does your partner describe their ideal life?

Does your partner have a significant health or career goal?

What is your partner hoping to become better at in the next 3 years?

What are the most important items on your partner's bucket list?

Does your partner have an achievable long-term goal?

<u>You and Me</u>

How did your partner realize that they liked you?

What does you partner miss most about you when you're apart?

What does your partner want most for you in the next three years?

Can you describe a time when your partner was proud of your relationship?

What activities or places does your partner love to do/visit with you?

_____

_____

_____

_____

_____

_____

_____

_____

<u>Other People</u>

Who is your partner's oldest friend?

Apart from you, who does your partner call to talk about their problems?

Who does your partner see as a role model?

Who is your partner's closest relative? How do they stay in touch?

Does your partner see themselves as sociable? Is it true?

<u>Careers</u>

What is your partner's position at work?

What is your partner best at in their position?

What part of the job does he/she like best? Least?

How, besides money, how do they feel rewarded by their work?

What are your partner's work friends like?

_____

_____

_____

_____

_____

_____

_____

Feelings

How does your partner unwind at the end of the day?

What makes your partner feel truly joyful?

Does your partner consider themselves content?

What do you do to make your partner feel happy?

_____

_____

_____

_____

_____

_____

_____

_____

10 Signs That You're Ready for Marriage

It seems the stars are aligning and its clearly time to settle down. Your friends are pairing off and you really believe you're ready to be in that number. But wait a second, is this simply peer pressure? Do you really want to spend the rest of your life with your current partner? Check out these signs and see if you're heading in the right direction?

1.   You know why you want to get married.

When you think about getting married you know exactly why you want it. Despite the pictures of tuxedos and white dresses all over your Facebook feed you've asked yourself the tough questions. Is that what you *really* want? Do you just want to be able to say, you're married, or do you really want a committed life with your partner? What benefits will you get from getting married compared to continuing the relationship as it is? The answers to *these* questions are what's leading you to marriage.

2. You're not simply planning a wedding, you're planning your marriage

You understand that the extravagant wedding is a nice one-day affair that ends with a magnificent party with family and friends. But you know that this can't be the reason to get married. The big party and being the center of attention will only last a few hours, but your marriage last forever. (Hopefully!) You're planning for the rest of your life. The contours and content of that life is where your major planning is. You're looking forward to a magnificent everyday life with your partner, when you're not necessarily the center of attention.

3.   You're living a grown-up life.

While it's true some high school sweethearts marry and make it work. It's not universal. Even studies show that for best outcomes you should wait until you're at least 25 to get married. But age is not the central factor, maturity is. You know you're not a kid anymore. You're not moving in this direction to please your parents or impress your friends. You have a life and an identity. You have pursuits and goals. You're mature, building a future of your own. Getting married would add to it, not create it.

4.   Your relationship is deep.

When love began, it was a fairy tale. You and your partner flirted, laughed and went out A LOT. No heavy conversations or unpleasant moments. Everything was unicorns and rainbows. But now something's different. Your relationship is more than just fun--- its deep. More than going out on the town or feeling lighthearted, your relationship is now about supporting your partner when they need you most. It's working through tense moments instead of shutting down. In this relationship you are present. You both have become thoughtful, deliberate…deep.

5.   You really know and trust your partner.

It's fair to say that you may never completely know anybody; no matter how many years you've been around them. In marriage, learning the secret quirks and habits of your partner, keeps everyone on their toes. And, in this relationship you've learned their hopes and dreams. You can predict with odd accuracy your partner's reaction to things. You trust them. There's a greater level of comfort that has grown between you two. You know their character and feel comfortable relying on them. Your desire to get married is not because you've been dating for a while or even because you're in love. You want to marry them because you've read their "fine print: and **know** this is the person for you.

6.   You have no desire to "change" your partner.

Not only do you know and trust your partner, you accept them. They are who they are, and you get that. You understand that making a major commitment won't change anyone nor do you want it to. You recognize that the only thing commitment may do is encourage you to work harder on your relationship. You don't expect a marriage to reinvent your relationship or the person in it with you. You love *them*…. warts and all.

7.   You resolve conflicts together.

You don't gloss over your problems. Together you've learned that forgetting problems won't make them better. You work out the kinks head on. The two of you do your best to avoid random blow ups. And you don't believe that marriage is the answer to problems. You work out any issues, because you and your partner communicate effectively. You both believe that resolving problems and compromising in a relationship is a strong foundation for a healthy marriage.

8.   You have mutual long-term plans.

Early in the relationship, you guys were flying by the seat of
your individual pants. Many times, you changed things at the
last minute because, you didn't have to plan beyond the next
Saturday night date. Your life outside of that was completely
your own. Now you're serious and deciding to commit to
each other. You know that you need to make plans together.
What if your partner wants to travel the world? Maybe you'd
like to go with, maybe not. Whether it's living Cali or
Kansas, having kids or puppies, plans are now a team effort.
You know for sure that whatever the future holds you need to
decide together.

9.   Your family and friends accept your partner.

Yes, it's your relationship and nothing else matters
outside of the two of you… at least that's how you felt
in the beginning. Now a little time has passed, and
you've committed to this relationship. You've come to
realize that *everything* matters. It's not about anyone's
approval, it's about creating a support system to help
transform your partnership into a family. You
understand that seemingly small rifts can affect your life
and your relationship. You don't want you or your
partner to be alienated from friends or family or to miss
important events. You're comfortable considering the
opinions of people you trust and respect.

10.   You know that this relationship has changed your life.

You know you're in love, but more than that, every scenario you imagine has your partner in it. You can't see yourself with anyone else. You can't see yourself without your partner either. Whatever twist or turn your life may take you know that you'd be incredibly unhappy without them along for the ride. Commitment no longer feels like bondage, it feels like the only thing that can truly set you free. You know it's time for marriage. It's time to take the plunge!

Marriage: Preparing Mentally

The beautiful institution of marriage comes with many obvious and wonderful changes. But it also changes your life in ways you may not necessarily anticipate. Any couple married longer than the honeymoon, can attest that some adjustments will come as a surprise, but still fall under the category of workable. Then there will be others that will flat out blow your mind. Beyond the beauty and romance, marriage is an institution powered by intentional effort. In marriage, you must consciously work toward accepting your spouse and all the surprises that may arise. So, now is the time to mentally prepare for the life that will soon unfold.

Understanding Your Partner

A good marriage results when two people really understand each other. Learning your partner's strengths and weaknesses and accepting them is invaluable. Learning what your partner values will help you gain a deeper understanding of who they are. Learn what truly makes them happy and what truly hurts. In general, women feel connected by talking, while men prefer doing things together. This may not apply to your spouse so be open and make real efforts to find out.

Adjusting Your Time

In marriage there is a merging of two individuals to form one unit. Each of you will bring love and a sense commitment to that unit but both of you will also bring a set of priorities and goals too. As a married person those things will require a different flexibility. Your routine, work time, even your sleep habits will need adjusting. You will have to consider the time and priorities of your partner, as well as make time for each other. The sooner the better.

Family Values and Lifestyle Differences

Keep in mind that every household is different. During dating, those differences seem like trivial variances, but in setting up your kingdom, those little nuisances can become very important. In marriage, you must keep an open mind. "Bizarre" in your eyes may be "tradition" in theirs. Recognize that it's important to observe, listen and respond without judgment. Give each other the gift of comfort in your own home. Respect your partner's family and show them genuine love. Connect well with their friends. Integration is smoothest when both parties feel valued.

There's No Place Like Home

Managing a household is a skill that requires mastery. From managing the household budget to paying the bills; your household will need to develop a rhythm. This rhythm will include making purchases, keeping it clean and customs as mundane as taking out the garbage and checking the mail. Establishing this process is a must for both husband and wife. Mastering you home will bring it much needed stability.

Managing Your Money

Together you and your partner must discuss a plan for a successful financial life. This plan must include monthly expenses, housing, insurance, travel, medical expenses and even outstanding debts. Be honest about your finances and expenses with your spouse. Trust is essential in this area.

MARRIAGE COUNSELING

Marriage Counseling helps married couples recognize and resolve conflicts and improve their relationships. Some couples seek Marriage Counseling to strengthen their partnership and gain a better understanding of each other.

Through Marriage Counseling, problem areas are revealed, while thoughtful strategies to rebuild and strengthen the relationship are formulated. In some cases, Marriage Counseling identifies serious issues where it may be more beneficial for the health and/or safety of both parties to go their separate ways.

Marriage Counseling can address
        Communication problems
        Anger
        Conflicts about child rearing or blended families
        Infidelity
        Sexual difficulties

In cases of domestic abuse and substance abuse, Marriage Counseling can be helpful to couples as they seek other appropriate therapies; while maintaining that crisis and physical violence requires emergency support.

As almost all marriages begin with high expectations, Marriage Counseling addresses issues from various sources that undermine those expectations. These issues can be grouped into three major categories: Surprises, Undermining Influences and Jolts.

Surprises include unfulfilled expectations, disappointing sex, faulty communications, unhealthy relationships, unwise choices, and secrets.

Undermining Influences that sneak up on a couple and harm the marriage include busyness, role confusion, inflexibility, religion, value differences, conflicting needs, personality differences, debt and money issues, boredom and weakening emotional bond.

Jolts to marriage include unexpected medical crisis, a sudden death, a discovered infidelity, a natural disaster, a deep disappointment, a financial or career collapse, or any other crisis that can throw a family into turmoil and severely shake the stability of even the best of marriages.

For Spiritual Support:

Can two walk together except they be agreed?
Amos 3:3

Marriage is honorable in all, and the bed undefiled: but whoremongers
and adulterers God will judge.
Hebrews 13:6

But whoso committeth adultery with a woman lacketh understanding:
he that doeth it destroyeth his own soul.
Proverbs 6:32

Charity suffereth long, and is kind; charity envieth not; charity
vaunteth not itself, is not puffed up,
Doth not behave itself unseemly, seeketh not her own, is not easily
provoked, thinketh no evil;
Rejoiceth not in iniquity, but rejoiceth in the truth;
Beareth all things, believeth all things, hopeth all things, endureth all
things.
Charity never faileth: but whether there be prophecies, they shall fail;
whether there be tongues, they shall cease; whether there be
knowledge, it shall vanish away.
I Corinthians 13:4-8

7 Reasons to Seek Marriage Counseling

Many commentaries assert that marriage is on the decline. It's often repeated that 50% of all marriages end in divorce, but that is an oversimplification. The truth is divorce levels vary greatly based on many factors such as education, religious beliefs and economic status. All things considered divorce rates have

remained relatively steady of the last 30 years.

However, divorce is a reality. The breakdown of a couple can be a very difficult for them, but in a marriage, it doesn't just affect the couple. It affects their children and creates schisms in those that have become their extended families.

Divorce is a stressful process that often begins with ambivalence and uncertainty about the future. It engenders feelings of guilt, shame, anger and blame. If children are involved, they may experience those feelings and may additionally develop a preoccupation with reconciling their parents.

In the end, divorce may prove to be the safest, healthiest option for some couples, but others may in fact choose to salvage their union. In those cases, when couples acknowledge that they are having difficulties, but may wonder when it's appropriate to seek marriage counseling. Here are 7 signs:

1.   Communication is Mostly Negative.

No matter what you say, its wrong. That is a common complaint with couples who are having difficulties. It's hard to turn a corner once communication has soured. Not only are the words in dispute, even the tone of voice can become a problem.

Not only can verbal communication be an issue, so can nonverbal communication. Silence, facial expressions, interjections like clearing your throat to interrupt or coughing to relay disbelief; as well as other non-words like grunts and sighs can make communicating nearly impossible. Negative communication can lead to hurt feelings and more gravely, abuse. Communication is vital in any successful relationship. When communication is the problem, you need to seek outside, unbiased help.

2.   When One or Both Partners Has Had or is Considering An Affair

An affair is one of the deepest violations of the boundaries of a marriage. It can be very difficult to recover, but not impossible. Recovery would require lots of work. Commitment and a willingness to move forward is key. Both individuals must be committed to a process of openness and honesty to salvage their marriage. Expert help can allow a couple to look directly at the issues involved in that very personal breach. Then clear decisions can be made concerning the sustainability of the marriage and whether or not to move on.

3.   **You've Become Roommates**

One of the most basic features of marriage is intimacy. It distinguishes marriage from most relationships and is an implied requirement, something unique to marriage. One of the clearest indications of the need for counseling is when a couple begins simply "occupying the same space". There is a lack of communication, conversation, sex and other elements that's important to couples. They just co-exist. This is an indication that skilled assistance is needed.

4.   **You Know What's Wrong, but Not How to Fix It**

You both know something is wrong. You've really tried communicating about it. Unfortunately it seems that these conversations only lead to rehashing old wounds over and over, solving nothing. When couples experience discord, recognize it, but can't do anything about it, it's time for expert help. In those situations, a skilled counselor can help guide and redirect couples who are stuck.

5.   **Someone has Begun to Act Out**.
Living in an unhappy or difficult situation can be frustrating. Feelings of sadness, disappointment and resentment are inevitable. It's possible to mask these feelings for a while, but eventually they can come to the surface. Then counterproductive behaviors begin to appear. Behaviors can range from passive-aggression, being late for an event very to your spouse because you "can't be bothered". To cutting up your spouse' clothing after an argument. When one or both of you begin acting out, it definitely time to get help.

6.   Separation Seems Like the Only Option

Couples may find when they argue a break can be helpful. They take a moment to calm down and compose themselves. Afterward, revisiting the issue can have a more productive outcome. But when the "cooling off" period becomes overnight stays away from the home, you're entering dangerous territory. The pattern of only being able to resolve a situation after an absence, leads to more absences. Eventually, the "cooling off" period becomes avoidance and it seems that there is only peace when you are away from each other. At this point, help is needed.

7.   You're Together for the Children

Often couples feel staying together for the children is the right thing to do. However, this is actually detrimental to them. It teaches them to expect from marriage what they see modeled in front of them. They may learn that marriage is an unhappy institution or that you shouldn't expect togetherness or warmth from your partner. They may learn it's easier to live in fear, than to face tough issues to resolve difficult challenges. These are not the lessons loving parents want to relay to their children. Children are intuitive and no matter how you try to hide it, they recognize the difference between tolerance and cohesion. Couples must commit to working though their issues for the sake of their children. Finding out if the relationship is healthier apart or salvageable is what you should do for your children. Skilled counseling can help.

Marriage can be a wonderful institution, but it is riddle with tests and challenges. It requires diligence and commitment. Some of those challenges unearth issues that make you wonder if continuing in your marriage is the wisest idea. Marriage counseling can help you work through issues honestly and impartially.

5 Signs That Your Marriage is Toxic: And What to Do

Toxic marriages are usually characterized by overt bad behavior like physical or verbal abuse and infidelity. But it is very possible to be in a toxic relationship, know that something is wrong but not be able to put your finger on it.

Toxicity in a marriage is very serious. It can make you feel distraught, depressed, depleted and drained. It can be the precipitous to chaos and really bad behavior. However, toxic relationships are not hopeless. With the appropriate counseling and commitment, even these relationships can be turned around. One of the keys to success is identifying toxicity and getting the appropriate help as soon as possible. Here are 5 signs to help:

1. **You're Always Walking on Eggshells**

    Your spouse appears to have a "Jekyll/Hyde" personality. You don't know who they will be from one moment to the next. One moment they're happy, they're raging the next. They can be perfectly fine with a decision one day and the next outraged about it. These sporadic unpredictable swings keep you in a fight or flight state. You spend the majority of your time trying to anticipate this ire and you're exhausted.

2. **You're On the Defensive**

    Being on eggshells constantly, creates an expectation of inconsistency and unpredictability. In turn, you find yourself ready to defend yourself in every interaction. Conflict is especially difficult. You simply don't trust your spouse and are always prepared for the other shoe to drop. Unfortunately, defensiveness causes you to begin behaving in a toxic fashion as well. If you spouse approaches you with an issue of any kind, you react negatively. In addition to identifying toxicity in your spouse, it's important to also pinpoint *your* defensiveness and avoid unhealthy behaviors.

3.   You Feel Drained

Long gone are the days of simple easy everyday conversations. Now nearly every conversation is heavy if not completely heated. Things have become so strained that you dread having conversations with your spouse. Every interaction is now tedious. Now every time you walk away from your spouse, you feel like someone's completely drained your energy. Sometimes you even feel physically ill. Feeling drained on a consistent basis is a sure sign of toxicity.

4.   You're Not in Control

There are no healthy boundaries in your marriage. Your spouse appears to have the upper hand in your life. Whether it be communication, time or attention your spouse lords over everything. Your spouse even controls your relationships outside of your marriage, money and other resources. Their preference prevails.

Control may not be overt. It may be passive-aggressive or manipulative or under the radar.

5.   You're Depressed

Being in a toxic relationship can very easily lead to depression. You lose energy, passion for life or interest in things you used to enjoy. Depression can cause you to neglect your family, friends, job and even yourself. It can also lead you to harm others or yourself. Depression can also lead to suicidal ideation. If you're depressed get help as soon as possible.

What Can You Do?

If you've realized that your marriage is toxic there are things you can do.

First seek professional help. You need to the assistance of some who can help put your marriage on the road to recovery. Ideally both you and your spouse should attend. But if they choose not to accompany you, go anyway. In time they may change their mind, You'll be healthier no matter what.

Secondly, own your part. There may behaviors that you too have contributed to the toxicity in your marriage. Hold yourself responsible and change issues you can control. This does not mean that your spouse will do the same, but you can be sure that you will be healthier if you do.

Finally, remember God is difficult with you as you walk through this situation. He is with you. Stay in the Word of God and pray consistently. God will work even this out for your good.

Remember,
If you are in danger, exit the situation as soon as possible. Leave the environment and do your best to create a solid boundary. Contact law enforcement when appropriate. It may be difficult to take drastic measures, but it could save your life.

Marriage Check-Up

Name: _____

Date : _____

HABITS	That's me	That's my spouse	Neither
Night Owl			
Early Bird			
Watches too much TV			
Way too much social media			
Smokes/ drinks too much			
Does things on purpose to drive me crazy			
Hardly finishes anything			
Absolutely no bad habits			

HOUSEHOLD	That's me	That's my spouse	Neither
Leaves clutter everywhere			
Can't keep the car clean			
Rarely cooks			
Rarely does household chores			
Does most of the household chores			
Does most of the cooking			
Finishes the household projects			

FAMILY/IN-LAWS	That's me	That's my spouse	Neither
Doesn't discipline the kids enough			
Rarely helps me with the kids			
Disciplines the kids way too much			
A Momma's Baby			
A Daddy's Baby			
Thinks I hate their parents			
Generally takes their parents' advice over mine			
Gets way too much advice from family members			
Has a healthy boundaries with extended family			
Puts our nuclear family first			

COMMUNICATION	That's me	That's my spouse	Neither
Is a really good communicator			
Is a really good listener			
Sometimes speaks to me ways that are grumpy, unloving or disrespectful			
Dominates the conversation			
Gives the silent treatment			
Seems more interested in talking with others than me			
Keeps emotions bottled up too much			
Forgives, but never forgets			
Punishes me by tone, reaction or blowing up			
Insists on having the last word			

INTIMACY	That's me	That's my spouse	Neither
Feels deeply connected to my partner			
Always wants sex			
Never wants sex			
Withholds sex as punishment			
Has a problem with pornography			
Has a lot of relationship scars from the past that we can't get over			
Has deep intimacy with God			
Puts forth effort to keep intimacy enjoyable for both of us			

FINANCES	That's me	That's my spouse	Neither
Great with finances			
Stresses out way too much about money			
Shops too much			
Never wants to do anything special because it's too expensive			
Doesn't understand the need to save for the future			
Doesn't see the need to enjoy today			
Pulls out money EVERY TIME a preacher asks			
Not great with money but still wants to take the lead			
Not great with money so never tries to take the lead			

THOUGHTS:

_____

_____

_____

_____

_____

_____

_____

_____

_____

_____

_____

_____

_____

_____

_____

_____

_____

_____

_____

_____

GRIEF

Grief is a normal multifaceted response to significant loss. The loss can be of a person, object, or opportunity. This expression of deprivation and anxiety manifests in a variety of ways including through behavior, emotions, thinking, physiology, interpersonal relationships and spirituality.

Grief is both a universal and an intensely personal experience. Sadness and hurt are the common responses to loss. Significance personalizes experience and **deepens fragile** emotions. It is highly subjective and can only be quantified by the person experiencing it. As significance compounds loss, grief can grow to a point where the ability to manage becomes difficult and assistance is needed.

Grief Counseling aids a mourner as they move through the process of grieving. This process includes "reconstructing meaning" after the loss, untangling oneself from the person, thing or possibility of that which was lost and handling the emotional impact.

Grief Counseling covers "uncomplicated mourning"; the expressions of sorrow, feelings of loss, intense pain, loneliness, depression, denial, fantasy, even physical manifestations. It also covers complicated mourning where expressions of grief include uncomplicated mourning and extend into realms of grief that are prolonged, delayed, denied or otherwise intensified to the detriment of the mourner. Through patience and compassion Grief Counseling helps mourners facilitate healthy grieving and ultimately a return to normalcy.

For Spiritual Support:

Blessed are they that mourn: for they shall be comforted
Matthew 5:4

And God shall wipe away all tears from their eyes; and there shall be
no more death, neither sorrow, nor crying, neither shall there be any
more pain: for the former things are passed away.
Revelation 21:4

Weeping may endure for a night but joy cometh in the morning.
Psalm 30:5b

We are confident, I say, and willing rather to be absent from the body,
and to be present with the Lord.
II Corinthians 5:8

But I would not have you to be ignorant, brethren, concerning them
which are asleep, that ye sorrow not, even as others which have no
hope.
For if we believe that Jesus died and rose again, even so them also
which sleep in Jesus will God bring with him.
I Thessalonians 4:13-14

Coping With Grief and Loss

There's no right or wrong way to grieve, but there are healthy ways to get through the grieving process. These tips can help

What is Grief?

Grief is your natural emotional response to loss. It's the process of assessing loss and reordering identity thereafter. Grief is painful and can sometimes feel overwhelming. It is possible to experience many different, often unexpected, emotions during the process including, shock, anger, disbelief, guilt and profound sadness. There can also be significant physical effects as grief can disrupt your physical health. Loss of sleep, difficulty eating, or digesting food and difficulty processing information is common. The more significant the loss, the more significant the effects.

Coping with grief is usually thought as coping with the loss of a loved one but grief can include many other types of loss including:

> Losing a job
> Loss of health
> Loss of financial stability
> Divorce or loss of a relationship
> Miscarriage
> Retirement
> Death of a pet
> Loss of a dream/goal
> Loss of a friendship
> A loved one's serious illness
> Loss of safety after a trauma
> Selling a family home

Even small losses can trigger grief. Circumstances like graduating from college or moving away from home can trigger feelings of grief and loss. Grief is very personal and varies based on your personal attachment. Never feel ashamed about what affects you. Significance in relationships can be with people, pets or even things. It really depends on what is significant to you. It's very normal and healthy. Time can ease your sadness and help you come to terms with your loss. Eventually you will find meaning and move on with your life. And if you have difficulty during the grieving process, there are resources that can help you find healthy ways to cope with that pain.

The Grieving Process

Grieving is a highly individualized experience. How you grieve depends heavily on factors like personality and coping style. Other factors including life experience, spiritual beliefs and significance of loss play a part as well.

With grieving, healing takes time. This gradual process can't be forced or hurried. It's vital to remember **there is no normal timetable for grieving.** For some, grieving could take as little as a few weeks or months. For others it could reasonably take years to move on from the pain. It's important to be patient and allow the process to unfold naturally. Also beware of myths that may complicate it.

Grief: Facts vs Myths

Myth: Pain goes away faster when you ignore it.
Fact: Ignoring or suppressing pain only makes it worse in the long term. The only way to really heal is to face your grief and deal with it.

Myth: It's important to "be strong" after a loss.
Fact: There are no emotions that make you weak. When grieving, its normal to feel sad and to cry. You may also feel lonely or confused. You shouldn't put on a "brave face" or try to protect others. By acknowledging your true feelings, you are in a better position to help yourself and others move forward.

Myth: If you don't cry. You're not really grieving
Fact: Crying is definitely a normal response to sadness, but not the only one. Depth of pain is not measured by crying. Those who don't cry may have other ways of showing it.

Myth: Grieving lasts about a year.
Fact: There is NO timetable for grief. Length of time truly varies from one person to the next.

Myth: Going on with your life means you've forgotten your loss.
Fact: Moving on, in no way implies that you've forgotten your loss. But it is an indication of the very healthy response of acceptance. It is a healing response to accept your loss and keep their memory as a cherished part of your life.

How to Deal with the Grieving Process

Grieving a loss is an unavoidable part of life. The process is deliberate and personal, but there are ways to cope that make it easier to find your way and move forward with life. They include:

    Acknowledge your pain.

    Realize that grief can trigger a range of unexpected emotions

    Remember that the grieving is unique to you it may not look like what you expect

    Seek face to face support from people who care about you

    Practice self-care both physically and emotionally

    Recognize that there is a difference between grief and depression

    If you're depressed seek help

The Stages of Grief

The Stages of Grief is based on the studies of terminally ill patients. The studies found sentiments common in individuals experiencing grief and loss. They have been progressively generalized to encompass negative life changes and losses including death of a loved one.

The Stages of Grief Are:

Denial: Feeling that the circumstance or diagnosis is in error. "This isn't really happening"

Anger: Frustration at the realization that the circumstance is real. "Why is this happening!"

Bargaining: Feeling like the situation can be avoided by negotiating. "I'll change if you save me"
Depression: Recognizing that there's nothing you can do and sinking into despair. "I'm too sad to bother doing anything"

Acceptance: Remembering that in life things happen and mortality is inevitable. This stage usually comes with calm and peace. "It's going to be okay".

Experiencing these emotions following a loss is expected but remember this is not a rigid framework and its possible not to experience all of them. You may also experience the stages of grief in a varied order or not at all. If your experience is different don't worry. The purpose of this research was to help those suffering understand in some part what they were experiencing while grieving. It is a resource and may help you as well.

Grief: A roller coaster

Instead of stages, maybe think of the grieving process as a roller coaster. It's filled with ups and downs, highs and lows. Like roller coasters, the ride tends to be rough at the beginning and the lows feel deep and long. There are good days where you're at the top of the roller coaster and bad days when it feels like you're rushing into the abyss. But stay on the ride. Difficult times will become less intense and shorter. Eventually the pain will subside.

Symptoms of Grief

Though grief affects people in very different ways, many experience the following similar symptoms. Be mindful that the in the early stages of grief anything is possible. You may feel like you're having a nervous breakdown or a heart attack. You may feel stuck in a bad dream or question deeply held religious beliefs. All of this is normal and will pass.

Emotional Symptoms

Shock and Disbelief: Immediately after a loss, it may be hard to accept what's happened. You may feel numb or are unable to process the truth. In the case of the death of a loved one, you may repeatedly expect them to come home, even though you know they're gone.

Guilt: It's very normal to feel guilt or regret after a loss. You may regret what you said or didn't say. You may feel guilty that you survived, and they didn't. Sometimes after a death, there's regret for feeling a sense of relief after a long difficult illness or that you didn't save that person, even when there was nothing they could do.

Sadness: Despair is a the most universal symptom of grief. You may have feelings of sadness, emptiness, yearning or deep loneliness. Some cry or feel emotionally unsteady.

Anger: Frustration, anger and resentment are traits of grief, even if it's no one's fault. The loss may feel so unjust, that you feel the need to hold someone or something responsible. People blame God, other people, the doctor or even the person who died.

Fear: A significant loss can trigger fear and worry. You may begin to evaluate everything around you and feel helpless, anxious or insecure. You may even have panic attacks. A death can trigger fears about your own mortality or the weight of facing life without them.

Physical Symptoms of Grief

Grief is not only an emotional experience, is a physical one as well. Symptoms include:

> Fatigue
> Lowered Immune system
> Weight loss or gain
> Aches and pain
> Insomnia

Support for Grief and Loss

Even if you're uncomfortable talking about your feelings under normal circumstances, as you grieve having someone to talk to is invaluable. Support especially face to face support is vital in healing from loss. Sharing your loss can make the burden of grief easier to bear. It will also help you to resist the temptation to withdraw from people and isolate yourself in your grief. The pain of grief may compel you to retreat into your shell but lean on you support system.

Turn to family or friends. Now is the perfect time to lean on the people who care about you. Draw close to the people who know and love you. Often people want to help but don't know how, so let them know that you need them. Let them help you if you have responsibilities regarding the loss, like funeral arrangements. Spend time with loved ones face to face. Cry on their shoulders if need be. If you don't have any close family or friendships, it's never too late to build new relationships.

Accept that people may feel awkward when trying to comfort someone. Grief is a very complicated emotion. Sometimes people have trouble trying to navigate the sea of emotions to console someone else, especially if they have not experienced a similar loss. Don't hold it against them or use it as an excuse to retreat into your shell. Remember if they reached out, they care.

Take comfort in your faith. If spiritual practices are meaningful to you take comfort in them. Spiritual activities such as prayer, meditation or going to church can be very helpful during the grieving process and can offer solace. If you're questioning your faith after your loss, talk to your clergyman or someone else in your religious community.

Join a support community. Grieving can feel very lonely. Sometimes sharing sorrow with others who have experienced similar loss, rather than a loved one. Bereavement support resources can be located through hospitals, hospices, funeral homes and counseling center.

Talk to a therapist or grief counselor. In times when it feels like your grief is too much to bear, talk to an experienced grief counselor. A counselor can support you and help you work though intense emotions and other obstacles to your grieving.

Use social media for grief support. Memorial pages and other social media sites have become very popular and can connect you to an audience worldwide that may share your experience. This can be a source of support and a very practical way to disseminate information like funeral plans. People can also post tributes and condolences of their own. These pages can be comforting.
However, be careful not to post sensitive information on a social media site. Also be mindful that sometimes well- meaning strangers may post inappropriate comments or advice. And internet trolls are also a concern. Creating a private page or a closed group can alleviate some of those concerns.

Practice Self-Care As You Grieve

Face your feelings. In order to heal, you must acknowledge your pain. Suppressing your grief may work for a while, but you can't avoid it forever. Avoiding the feelings of sadness and loss only prolongs the grieving process. In order to heal you must face it or it can lead to depression, anxiety, substance abuse and other health problems.

Find tangible or creative ways to express yourself. Write a journal. Start a scrapbook or photo album. Write a letter to the person that you've lost saying all the things you didn't have a chance to say. Join a cause or organization that was important to your loved one. These creative outlets will allow you honor and remember, as well as cope with grief in a very healthy way.

Look after your physical health. Grief effects the body and the mind, because they are connected. When you're physically healthy you feel more emotionally healthy. Fight the stress and fatigue of grief by eating right and exercising. This will help boost your mood naturally. Avoid alcohol and drugs which may temporarily numb pain, but it very soon makes it worse.

Don't let anyone tell you how you feel. Your grief is unlike anyone else's. No one can tell you to when to move on or get over it. Indulge your feelings as deeply or as long as you need to. Don't let anyone stifle you and don't stifle yourself.

Plan for triggers. Over time you will begin to heal and feel better. But be aware that anniversaries, holidays, and other milestones may reawaken both memories and feelings associated with your loss. Create strategies to face those feelings and possibly honor the person you loved.

When Grief Doesn't Go Away

The grieving process is a gradual process but eventually the sorrow and hurt usually eases. The negative emotions should become more intense as you come to accept the loss and start moving forward. However, if your symptoms are in fact getting worse you may be developing a much more serious issue, complicated grief.

Complicated Grief

The hurt of losing someone can be intense and jolting but overtime it should significantly diminish. But if it remains the center of your existence and prevents you from resuming your life, then you may be suffering with complicated grief.

Complicated Grief is when you become stuck in a state of mourning. You have trouble accepting the loss and become so preoccupied with it that it takes over your life. It undermines your relationships and interrupts your routine.

Symptoms of Complicated Grief are:
Intense yearning for your deceased loved one
Denial of death or a sense of disbelief
Intrusive thoughts and/or images of your loved one
Imagining that your loved one is alive
Feeling empty or meaningless
Extreme anger or bitterness
Avoiding things that remind you of your loved one
Searching for them in familiar places.

If your loss was sudden, violent or extremely stressful complicated grief can manifest as psychological trauma or PTSD. You may feel helpless and struggle with negative emotions, memories and anxiety that won't go away. In this case, you should seek a skilled professional to help guide through the process and back into your own life.

When to seek professional help for grief

If you experience symptoms of complicated grief or clinical depression seek mental treatment right away. Left untreated these conditions can lead to significant emotional damage, life threatening health problems and suicide. Contact a counselor if you:
Feel life isn't worth living
Wish you had died with your loved one
Blame yourself for not preventing the loss
Feel numb or disconnected for more than a few weeks
Don't trust people since the loss
Can't perform normal daily duties anymore

GRIEF

How Our Dreams Heal Us

Who among us has not wished for that one final opportunity to see a deceased loved? Seems impossible, but maybe not. This can and often does happen in our dreams. Dreams of loved ones are very common.

We know how important dreams are to our overall health, but they may also play a role in the grieving process. During the day, we can be distracted by the noise of the day, but when we're asleep, we're relaxed and open. The subconscious mind is free to roam and process however it pleases.

A 2014 study in the American Journal of Hospice and Palliative Care examined the impact of grief related dreams on the bereaved and found that dreams of the deceased occurred frequently and can be highly meaningful and further healing from loss.

Themes in those dreams included, past memories, the deceased free from illness, the deceased in the afterlife appearing healthy, comfortable and at peace as well as the deceased sending a message. Respondents found the dreams were helpful in accepting death. Grief counseling was still recommended to aid in the healing process.

Studies show that dreams tend to vary based on where the mourner is in the grieving process, how long the loved one's been gone, the relationship with them and how they died. Research shows that there are four common dreams:

Visitation, when the loved one simply spends time with you

Message dream, here the deceased appears with information or to say I love you

Reassurance dream, when they come to comfort

Trauma dream, reliving a disturbing event like murder or an accident

Grief dreams are not limited to these four types and most often are a combination of many different elements. Visitation dreams during a long illness is a theme that arises frequently. Goodbye dreams just prior to or right after the death are common as well.

In essence, all grief dreams are visits from our loved ones. They feel different from typical dreams in that they are reported to feel very real. The deceased is usually whole and healthy again. They bring messages of hope and reassurance. Sometimes they bring warnings and guidance.

Dreamers describe the communication as almost telepathic in that no words are exchanged but much information is communicated. These dreams tend to arouse very strong feelings in the dreamer, but they ultimately wake more able to cope with the loss of their loved one. The dreams can also be spiritually transformative for the dreamer. While some attribute the dreams to wish fulfillment, others believe that they have in fact had a true spiritual experience.

Grief dreams rarely need any interpretation as they speak for themselves. They are a normal part of grieving; they soothe and comfort and have the ability to help mourners to heal.

Grief in Men

When they're young men don't face much personal loss, but once they reach a certain age, they will in fact experience a significant loss be it a spouse or a close friend. Grief will naturally follow. Unfortunately some men are less prepared for the strong emotions that accompany that process and will tend to struggle. A little guidance on what to expect can help.

Effects on the Body and Mind

Doctors classify grief into two types: acute and persistent. Acute grief occurs in the first six to 12 months after a loss but gradually resolves. Persistent grief is grief that lasts longer than 12 months.

During a period of grief, you may become engrossed with thoughts, memories, and images of the one you lost. You may have difficulty accepting the finality of the loss and feel waves of sadness and yearning. Men may suddenly feel vulnerable and begin to sense their mortality.

Chronic stress also is normal during acute grief and can lead to physical and emotional issues. Some of which are depression, insomnia, anger and bitterness, anxiety, loss of appetite, and aches and pains. Men may try to resist the emotions associated with grief, but it's essential not to ignore these symptoms. Constant stress puts you at a greater risk for heart attack, stroke, and even death.

Those who experiencing persistent grief should definitely obtain a therapist or counselor to help with grieving process.

Coping with grief

A specially designed eight-week mind-body program can help reduce stress in older adults who have lost a spouse.

These are the main components of the program that can help you when dealing with acute grief.

Take up yoga, tai chi, or qigong. Not only can these mind-body activities help you relax, but they can reverse the effects of stress and anxiety on a molecular level. In people who consistently engaged in these practices, less inflammation in the body. Many classes are intended especially for stress reduction. You can attend classes online or at a local yoga studio or community centers.

Retain a healthy diet. Stress triggers cravings for sugar and fat, Yet in the end these foods can make you feel worse. Instead, focus on a well-balanced diet. This means plenty of vegetables, fruits, and lean proteins. And don't forget plenty of water.

Get plenty of sleep. Grief is emotionally exhausting. After a loss, people often find that their sleep is interrupted. They have trouble falling asleep, wake up in the night, or sleep way too much. Avoid alcohol and caffeine and follow a consistent bedtime for a more restful sleep.

Get moving. A daily walk can help reduce depression, agitation, and sorrow associated with grief. When you're grieving it can be difficult to find the energy to exercise. If you need motivation, ask a workout buddy to join you or become a member of an exercise group.

Keep up with your health. When grieving it's easy to ignore your general health. Do your best not to miss doctor's visits or your medications. Set reminders for any appointments or medications in advance to help keep you on schedule.

Reach out to the people who love you. Initially it may be difficult to see people, you must maintain connections with others. During the grieving process you must remember that you are not alone, and even if you feel isolated. There may be family members, friends, or even neighbors who would love to give a supportive hand. Have lunch or coffee weekly with someone or invite people over for a monthly potluck. Make an effort to communicate with someone every day

SECTION II

For Spiritual Support:

Peace I leave with you, my peace I give unto you: not as the world giveth, give I unto you. Let not your heart be troubled, neither let it be afraid.
John 14:27

Thou wilt keep him in perfect peace, whose mind is stayed on thee: because he trusteth in thee.
Isaiah 26:3

He that dwelleth in the secret place of the most High shall abide under the shadow of the Almighty.
I will say of the Lord, He is my refuge and my fortress: my God; in Him will I trust.
Surely, He shall deliver thee from the snare of the fowler, and from the noisome pestilence.
He shall cover thee with His feathers, and under His wings shalt thou trust: His truth shall be thy shield and buckler.
Thou shalt not be afraid for the terror by night; nor for the arrow that flieth by day;
Nor for the pestilence that walketh in darkness; nor for the destruction that wasteth at noonday.
A thousand shall fall at thy side, and ten thousand at thy right hand; but it shall not come nigh thee.
Only with thine eyes shalt thou behold and see the reward of the wicked.
Because thou hast made the Lord, which is my refuge, even the Most High, thy habitation;
There shall no evil befall thee, neither shall any plague come nigh thy dwelling.
Proverbs 91:1-10

TRAUMA, TERROR, AND TERRORISM

Terror: *The state of intense or extreme fear.*

Terrorism: *The deliberate use of force or violence by individuals or groups to instill extreme fear and exercise control over others.*

Trauma: *The intense stress, physical or psychological, that disrupts stability.*

Trauma, Terror and Terrorism are three words that can carry loaded meaning for individuals varying in significance and symbolism. They can be extremely subjective in view and import. Some quibble over whether terrorism *is* terrorism if the use of force is sanctioned by some lawful pronouncement or body. Then the question, becomes which authorities are lawful and which are not. Many domains have sanctioned activities under the guise of permission, not necessarily commission. Even the United States of America has a history of "allowing" extrajudicial activities as a means of creating fear and/or compliance in certain groups. Whatever the case, one thing is certain, the effects of extreme fear on the body, mind and spirit are undeniable.

Trauma, Terror and Terrorism conjure and exacerbate deepest fears real and imagined. Once thought of as the plight of those somewhere far away, outside of civil society; this triune nemesis has become an increasingly formidable condition in this modern era. The three words are even a "catch all" in some environments. They are used to stoke the basest responses from victims and often leave those experiencing them in a state of great perpetual anxiety.

In Christian Counseling, it is imperative that Trauma, Terror and Terrorism be clearly defined, identified and treated. Because unlike generations past, we are surrounded by a world of terror impacted people every day and the lasting effects are persistently surfacing.

Biblical Reference:

While there is no direct reference to the *word* Trauma in the Bible, Trauma as it is experienced and defined by both the medical and military communities can be found throughout. As early as the Book of Genesis in the Garden of Eden, Adam and Eve experienced the Trauma of the power of lies and propaganda. While Satan did not use physical violence to have his way, the force of his duplicity shook the very foundation of trust that had been all they knew up unto that point. So much so that it elicited a response of distrust and disobedience to a Person who had been nothing but trustworthy in their experience. This type of Terrorism has been repeated over and over in countless circumstances. Trust shaken can be a powerful weapon against the vulnerable. Additionally, the consequences thereafter had to once again shake them to their core. Pain and hardship were introduced into the lives of people who had no concept of them. Fear of the Unknown was born in that moment. It so Traumatized Adam and Eve that according to scientist the injury called Fear of the Unknown is a phenomenon that lives in the physiology of every one of their human descendants (Philip Toyote, 2015).

The word Terror, however, does appear in the Bible on many occasions. It appears during wars and captivities; approaching adversaries and in crises of conscious. Deuteronomy 32:25, most succinctly summaries the condition of man; "The sword without and terror within, shall destroy both the young man and the virgin, the suckling also the man of gray hairs. Terrorism is a feature of both our adversary the devil, (I Peter 5:8) and wicked people (Ephesians 2:2-3). The use of force; be it physical force, spiritual force or psychological force is always a risk we face. But I Peter 3: 12-14 reminds Christians that the Lord is for us and "against those that do evil". As such, we should not fear their Terrorism. And the peace of God which passes all understanding shall guard our hearts and mind through Christ Jesus. (Philippians 4:7)

The Causes of Terror and Terrorism

All the ways of a man are Clean in his OWN eyes (Proverbs 16:2)

The causes of Terror and Terrorism are often represented as complex. These "complexities" lie in the characterization of what activity is being engaged in and who is perceived as engaging it. The assumption is that the perpetrator is a youthful, brainwashed, destitute person with limited education and nothing to lose. Another prevailing thought is that only radicalized Muslims engage in activity that would be considered terrorism. Both assumptions are untrue.

Many of those engaged in terrorist activity are married, upper middle-class and educated. They leave communities, good families and stable jobs. They may or may not be religious radicals. And if they are, they may not be Muslim. All religious persuasions contain radical fringe elements including Christianity.

Terrorist are not suspicious looking strangers. They generally appear to be everyday people. One of the most significant features of modern Terrorism is the element of surprise. Most often society is not afforded the luxury of facing a Goliath day after day, warning and waiting. Though that too can be quite jolting.

While it may appear a capricious assemblage, seemingly unrelated groups like neo-Nazis, religious fundamentalists, anti-abortionist assassins, violent environmental protection groups, white nationalist, military regimes, corrupt policemen and organizations like al-Qaeda have very simple traits in common. They share an "us-vs-them" mentality and they truly believe they are RIGHT. It is this conviction of "righteousness" that leads to the internal justification that make all the horrors they inflict on others possible. The inclusion of ideology and or a charismatic leader exacerbates an already toxic stew. Unfortunately, it is also this justification that enables the dismissal of the Trauma their actions inflict.

Terror as a Consequence

There are instances in which a terrifying event is not one orchestrated to elicit a particular response, nonetheless the traumatic effect is the same. In cases of horrific accidents, sudden loss of loved ones or natural disasters people can experience feelings of terror so intense that there is a loss of internal equilibrium.

Following the events of Hurricane Katrina, many New Orleans residents reported feelings of depression, anxiety, nervousness, distrust and even anger. Hypervigilance was common, as was difficulty sleeping. Clearly, a hurricane is not a man-made event and the breaches that allowed flood waters to consume the City were not anticipated but those affected by them were traumatized and in need of counseling.

The victims of the California wildfires reported similar symptoms; as did victims of the tsunamis in Thailand. Traumatic events take on many forms and do not require bad actors.

Psychological Effects of Terrorism, Terror and Trauma

Fear is a natural response to unsafe unpredictable events or circumstances. It alerts the body and mind that some action needs to be taken and then folds that circumstance into an already established identity. Short term effects of trauma include fear, uncertainty, anger, and confusion. Other psychological defense mechanisms may surface but they often subside within minutes to days.

Some develop acute stress disorder (ASD). This disorder includes normal symptoms of trauma but also include a sense of detachment, a reduced awareness of one's surroundings, appearing dazed; feelings that the event is "unreal". The person may be emotionally unresponsive, confused, anxious and resist any attempts to contact persons or things that may remind them of the traumatic event. They will likely experience a heightened startle reflex, irritability, flashbacks and trouble sleeping. ASD is more common in instances of prolonged or highly intense traumatic events and can last for days or even weeks. ASD is more common in first responders and workers who have frequent contact with traumatic events.

PTSD

Post-traumatic Stress Disorder (PTSD)

When most people go through traumatic events temporary difficulty adjusting and coping can occur, but with time and good self-care, they usually get better. The body's ability to readjust is instinctual and resilient. However, there are circumstances when the symptoms get worse, last for months or even years, and interfere with day-to-day functioning, at this point is likely that the victim is experiencing Post-traumatic Stress disorder (PTSD)

PTSD can develop from seeing, going through or even learning about a traumatic event. It is unclear why some develop PTSD and others do not. Doctors theorize that a complex combination of stressful experiences and severity of trauma you've experienced; along with any personal mental health risks, temperament and the way your brain regulates the stress hormones and chemicals in the body all play a role in the emergence of the disorder.

PTSD has a three-pronged feature:

Recurring thoughts in the form of flashbacks and vivid dreams. Sometimes conflation of the event and the memory of the event occurs

Avoidance of people, places and things that could bring back a memory of the event. This avoidance can be unconscious. There may also be a refusal to discuss the event entirely.

Hyperarousal demonstrating as sleeplessness, poor concentration, frequent startle reactions, and a high alertness to ways of protecting self and loved ones.

PTSD is not the typical reaction to stress and traumatic events. It is a more serious, longer lasting set of invasive symptoms, but therapies and treatment can dramatically assist recovery.

Terror, Terrorism and Trauma and Neurobiology

The physiology of Terror, Terrorism and Trauma goes primarily through the brain. The shock of a traumatic event sends the body into high alert. The Limbic system tells the Hippocampus to stop functioning as usual and go into emergency mode. The Hippocampus, with the Amygdala sounding the alarm, send out neurohormones, including Adrenaline, to get the heart faster, causes the muscles to become tense and get ready for action and accelerates the breathing to supply more oxygen to the body. While all this activity is taking place in the Hippocampus, the Amygdala, the part of the Brain that controls emotion and memory is stuck waiting for the information to be pushed into the cerebral cortex for reasoning, understanding and logic. The limbic system is simply too busy processing the emergency.

Victims of traumatic events may have difficulty going past the event because the memory is still lodged in the limbic system and the signal never made it to the cerebral cortex. In other words, traumatic events continue to plague victims because the message that the danger is over has not been processed by the cerebral cortex and the signal hasn't made its way back to the memory center. The body simply doesn't know everything is ok. Stress reactions continue to recur in the brain and with every trigger, victims continue to suffer.

Counseling

Counseling survivors of Terror, Terrorism and Trauma requires a very patient inciteful multifaceted set of approaches. The *Rush to Debrief* should be the first thing to avoid. Though it may seem natural to a Counselor to immediately seek to try and open dialogue with a victim and stimulate as much recall as possible; the effect made actually trigger stress reactions as opposed to minimizing them. Allowing a victim to say as much as they choose to, is a more productive way to begin.

Immediately following a traumatic event the person will feel anxious and confused. And varying circumstances can illicit multiple supplementary responses. For example, victims of sexual abuse may feel feelings of shame or accident survivors may feel guilt, in addition to all the other feelings associated with a traumatic event. It is imperative that counselors provide a place of Safety, Trust and Reassurance. Calm and safety are the signals to the body that it needs to calm down. This calm will assist the reset needed to process and eventually overcome a traumatic event.

Use cognitive behavior therapies to help the person take more control of their thoughts and environments. Practices like time management and deep breathing used within this method has been shown to assist greatly with recreating a sense of normalcy and empowerment.

Counseling must include a neurobiological component. Whole Brain Techniques such as Story Telling and Multi-sensory Techniques that include music therapy and dance stimulate the whole body and engage both the mind and brain in resetting its normal sensory functions.

When engaging, counselors must remember to Recognize Group Differences. Though the human species is basically the same, humanity is influenced by social, cultural and geographical differences. Cross-cultural interventions contain many challenges. The ability to communicate effectively and respectfully within those parameters will require intention.

Of special importance are the belief systems of the victim; especially their perspective regarding healing. Healing and resilience are highly shaped by those systems and to be truly helpful, the counselor's focus should be assisting the victim back into them.

Counseling should also give victims Information and Coping Strategies, Stimulate Community Based Interventions to connect them with other spiritual, economic, social and or practical supports. These interventions can be key to relieving some of the aftermath stressors victims will face.

The entire process must emphasis Hope. Being lost in fear can leave one with a feeling of exhaustion and hopelessness. Be it the sheer horror of one explosive event or the consistent trickle of many small recurring events; Hopelessness is a feature of the inability to normalize the experience. Not seeing how it makes sense or how it could get better can trap a victim in a vicious cycle of distress and despair. But the victim must be reminded that things can get better. Believing this and taking affirmative steps toward healing will provide new possibilities.

Finally, practices that connect victims with God are the most effective tools, as He is the God of Comfort. And He will keep them in Perfect Peace whose mind is stayed on Him, because they trust Him. These connections must include other believers and supportive family members. But the most central focus must be on God, His nature and His power. Emphasis in prayer should be on consistence, peace and guidance; giving thanks even amid trauma. And the peace of God that passes all understanding, will guard their heart and mind for, there is nothing too hard for Him. Christian Counselors must remember that it is imperative that the foundation of all therapies be faith in God.

For Spiritual Support:

*For God hath not given us the spirit of fear; but of power, and of love,
and of a sound mind.*
II Timothy 1:7

*Finally, my brethren, be strong in the Lord, and in the power of his
might.*
*Put on the whole armour of God, that ye may be able to stand against
the wiles of the devil.*
*For we wrestle not against flesh and blood, but against principalities,
against powers, against the rulers of the darkness of this world, against
spiritual wickedness in high places.*
*Wherefore take unto you the whole armour of God, that ye may be able
to withstand in the evil day, and having done all, to stand.*
Ephesians 6:10-13

For though we walk in the flesh, we do not war after the flesh:
*(For the weapons of our warfare are not carnal, but mighty through
God to the pulling down of strong holds;)*
*Casting down imaginations, and every high thing that exalteth itself
against the knowledge of God, and bringing into captivity every thought
to the obedience of Christ;*
II Corinthians 10:3-5

MENTAL DISORDERS

Mental Illness: *Health conditions involving changes in emotion, thinking or behavior (or a combination of these).*

Mental Disorder or Psychiatric Disorder: a behavioral or mental pattern that causes significant distress or impairment of personal functioning. Such features may be persistent, relapsing and remitting, or occur as a single episode. Many disorders have been described, with signs and symptoms that vary widely between specific disorders.

Mental Disorders are a collective of mental conditions that describe the injured or damaged functions of the mind and by extension the behavior of a person. To fully grasp the impact of mental illness, one must first appreciate the significance of **mental health**.

Mental Health is the defined *as a state of well-being in which every individual realizes his or her own potential, can cope with the normal stresses of life, can work productively and fruitfully, and is able to make a contribution to her or his community. (World Health Organization, 2014)*

Mental Health touches every decision we make in life and influences not only how we experience the world, but how we contribute to the experiences of others. Mental Health is not the absence of stress or sickness. It is the ability to function fruitfully in every circumstance including those that may be uncomfortable. Measurements of specific impact are relative to environment, opportunity and individual cultural standards. However, that subjectivity does not obscure to the fact that a healthy mental state leads to better relationships, easier adaptations to life's fluctuations and overall quality of life. Mental illness disrupts one's ability to experience the benefits of that well-being.

Distress, Deviance, Disability and Dysfunction

Mental Disorders encompass a variety of different illnesses. Some of which manifest with very mild symptoms; others much more severe. But whether they be mood or behavioral disorders their emergence appears to several major categories **Distress, Deviance** and finally **Disability** and **Dysfunction**.

The **Distress** category includes Anxiety, Depression, Anger or other emotional suffering that is more psychological than physical. **Deviance** involves thinking or acting in ways that most people in society would consider unusual or inappropriate. **Disability** and **Dysfunction** both refer to illnesses that interfere with one' ability to handle daily routines, hold a job or converse clearly. These include phobias, personality disorders and deep depression.

The severity of any one of these illnesses run the gambit person to person. Many factors including biology can be determinative. Additionally, tolerance of the disruptions varies. Some can hide behavior or distress so well that the illness goes practically unnoticed, while others become so distressed that they become a danger to themselves and/or others.

Mental Disorders and the Bible

The Bible does not use the language of psychopathology. This election has at times been used in error to justify oversimplifying the suffering of mankind as demonic or simply sinful. Conditions such as epilepsy were thought of as demonic possession when in truth it was a neurological matter. However, the Bible's lack of explicit explanation of mental illness, does not negate its very thorough elucidation on the nature and suffering of man. And that suffering could in effect create conditions that effect man's ability to be fruitful.

The Bible speaks to minds becoming darkened and confused, the Prophet Elijah experienced what would in modern times be classified as suicidal ideation (I Kings 19:4-5), Nebuchadnezzar had what could only be seen as a nervous breakdown (Daniel 4:33) and in despair Judas Iscariot committed suicide (Matthew 27:5). These are only a few examples of the many situations that challenged the mental health of biblical citizens. The children of Israel are a virtual cornucopia of personality disorders from unstable kings to incestual episodes in a nation of moody subjects.

The Bible recognizes the Sin Nature of man as the primary point of origin for all the schisms of mankind, as should we, but this does not negate the healing virtue available to us through the finished work of Jesus Christ. And while some mental illness may in fact be the result of deliberate sin, not all psychopathology is.

Causes of Mental Disorders

Both the prevalence and types of mental illness are dependent on many different factors. Though overall mental disorders are spread evenly among men and women; the different genders tend to suffer more often from a different spectrum of illnesses. Women tend to suffer more from depression and phobias, while men tend to suffer more with drug and alcohol abuse and antisocial personalities.

But to be clear, these conditions do not arise from a set of simplistic prognostications. There are very real micro-variables that effect each situation uniquely. As with most circumstances, everyone brings a set of factors specific to their person. Biology, family history, culture and life experience all play a role in determining which conditions manifest and how the person suffering with it processes it. Despite these differences, all mental disorders arise from a combination of present stressors and past predisposing influences.

4 Categories of Present Stressors

A.   Biological Stress: Disease, the influence of drugs, toxins, or pollutants in the air, brain damage or physical deprivations such as lack of nutrients or sleep.

B.   Psychological Stress: Frustrations, feelings of insecurity, inner conflicts, fears or even pressure to get things done when you have too much to do. Disappointments also create stress as they engender a sense of loss and possibly the weight of not meeting other's expectations

C.   Social Stress: Economic uncertainty, wide-spread unemployment, political instability, or threat of terror attacks can be overwhelming for some. Tension and uncertainties even change in the physical environment such as prolonged darkness, heat waves, crowding or noise can make coping more difficult and increase the likelihood of mental disorders.

Types of Predisposing Influences:

A.   Biological Predispositions: Heredity, physical health, congenital defects, or other physical influences. Conditions like Depression may be stimulated by stress but can be exacerbated by the body's inability to adequately respond.

B.   Psychological Predispositions: Early family disharmony, childhood losses, parental neglect or abuse, faulty learning or previous rejection; even an upbringing that was too ridged can foster feelings of perpetual failure and further amplify the emergence of mental disorders.

C.   Sociological Predispositions: Issues such as social class, marital status, socioeconomic status, religious affiliation, and membership in a minority group. Access to resources and treatment lessen the prevalence of mental disorder, increase the likelihood and quality of treatment and lessen the likelihood of registration as a mental health statistic.

D.   Spiritual Predispositions: Abusive church experiences, involvement in satanic rituals, cultic activity or the residual effects of past blatant sinful behaviors. These issues can be impactful even in the life of the believer.

Locus of Control

The concept **Locus of Control** asserts that the influence of Present

Stressors and Predisposing issues can depend on how much control the person feels he or she has over the circumstances and directions of life. According to this theory, research has shown that people can have an internal or external locus of control.

Internal locus of control characterizes people who believe that what happens in life depends largely on their own decisions and actions. People with an external locus of control assume that the events in one's life depend on other people, luck or chance. Those with an internal locus of control tend to be mentally and physically healthier as they take proactive steps regarding events in their lives, probably because in life they have learned to be optimistic. The converse tends to be true of those with an external locus of control. They tend to give up trying.

Based on the finding that locus of control is largely learned psychologist proposed the theories of learned helplessness and learn optimism. People who have learned helplessness tend to be more depressed and have poorer health. In contrast people who begin to see that they can control their lives develop a sense of optimism and by extension have better mental health.

Though hotly debated, this core element remains, the impact of present stress and past influences is tempered according to how much a person feels in control of his or her life. Research has shown that the strong believer in God may have similarities to people with an internal locus of control. They operate from the premise that life is in control because God answers prayer and He honors our faith in submitting difficult problems to Him. Believers like everyone else can be overwhelmed by stress and past influencers, but a sense that everything is under control can help prevent mental disorders and the harmful impact of stress-inducing influences.

Sin and Responsibility

Some Christian Counselors hold the belief that mental disorder is mostly a result of personal deliberate sin. They utilize confession and repentance as the primary method of treatment. This short-sided view negates the complexity of mental disorders as well as the deeply penetrating influence of sin. Sin can be evaluated from two side perspectives, conscious deliberate sin and the innate sinfulness that is a part of human nature. These can be seen as the two sides of sin. Likewise, there can be two sides of responsibility, either person or someone else.

Mental Disorders and the Four Quadrants of the Influence of

Sin and Responsibility

I.   Mental Disorder due to deliberate sin committed by the person. Encouraging confession, change in behavior, learn new skills and getting help to prevent recurrence are among the most appropriate counseling strategies.

II.   Mental Disorder due to sin that originates with others. Examples include someone with great feelings of inferiority and low self-esteem that were the victim of constant put-downs by a teacher, parent or spouse or a woman who suffers a rape. Counseling may involve forgiveness, change in perceptions and learning to let go of long-standing hurts, bitterness and painful memories.

III.   Mental Disorders due to being pulled down deeply felt fears, insecurities, immaturities, ignorance, past traumas, inherited physical influences, harmful attitudes or other aspects of the personality that come because we live in a fallen world and are deeply affected by it. The Pharisees were an example of this, with righteous outward behavior and inner corruption that manifests in behaviors and thoughts that are harmful. Help in these circumstances come only with increased insight, confession and willingness to let God cleanse, change and mature the inner man. This kind of work take time and commitment.

IV.   Mental Disorders due to the sinful influence that permeates the culture. Conflict, stress, poverty, inequality, war, disease and widespread injustice are and will be a part of this culture until Christ's return and pathological responses to them will as well. Christians are responsible to resist social injustice, work for peace and strive to create a better world. Additionally, people must be taught how to cope with the stresses that give rise to pathology and help overcome the persisting effects of painful past experiences.

> Mental Disorders rarely come exclusively from only one of these four quadrants, but a combination. Though marginalized by mainstream psychiatry and psychology, the consideration of the influence of sin provides an important perspective to help in addressing mental disorders. Sin influence as a part of a

comprehensive approach by the Christian Counselor will provide an untapped trove of resources to assist a counselee.

The Effects of Mental Disorders

"Mental Illness is a major social problem that consumes millions of tax dollars; costs billions in lost wages, absenteeism, inefficiency, criminal behavior and expensive treatment". (Gary R. Collins, 2007) It effects individuals and families alike in numbers that provoke serious concern.

Approximately 1 in 5 adults in the U.S. (46.6 million) experiences mental illness in a given year. (National Institute of Mental Health, 2019)

Approximately 1 in 25 adults in the U.S. (11.2 million) experiences a serious mental illness in a given year that substantially interferes with or limits one or more major life activities. (National Institute of Mental Health, 2019)

Approximately 1 in 5 youth aged 13–18 (21.4%) experiences a severe mental disorder at some point during their life. For children aged 8–15, the estimate is 13%. (National Institute of Mental Health, 2019)

The Effects on Individuals

A.   Emotion

a.   Emotional intensity characterized by intense feelings of depression, anxiety, anger, guilt or other painful emotions

b.   Emotional variability characterized by unpredictable emotional "ups and downs".

c.   Flat effect characterized by a tendency to remain emotionless or express no feelings

d.   Inappropriate effect characterized by emotions that are either unprovoked or do not match situational circumstances such as giggling in response to sad news

B.   Sensation and Perception: The ability to receive and process sensory information

    a.   Enhanced sensitivity characterized by acute hearing, perceiving colors more as bright; an inability to relax or concentrate due to feeling overwhelmed by what is perceived as a flood if information at times there is difficulty sorting out and synthesizing sensations.

    b.   Distorted sensitivity characterized by misinterpreting stimuli and misperceiving the world. Delusions, hallucinations, and illusions are experienced and deeply held as beliefs by those who suffer with these types of mental illness

    c.   Thinking Difficulty: *Faulty thought content* where a person does not think clearly, logically, or consistently. Thought everyone experiences some faulty thinking they usually know or can be shown that the thinking is faulty. Those with mental disorders are unable or are unwilling to respond to objective argument or evidence. *Faulty thought progression,* another Thinking Difficulty, is characterized by rambling disconnected thoughts, easily interrupted thoughts, obsessive thinking or an inability to think abstractly.

Emotional and/or Sensational distortions have the capacity to manifest as crippling Mental Disorders.

Effects on Families

    Behavior that is perceived as inappropriate or unusually immature can be difficult for family members to be patient or understanding of. It can be difficult for them to cope with it. This can be complicated by the fact that mental disorders run in families and family care givers may be struggling with some form of psychological disorders similar to that member who needs care.

Families differ but typically go through a series of phases before seeking to assist the family member in need of treatment. First, they ignore or explain away; then they recognized the first shock of behavior that can't be ignored; next withdrawal and reevaluation in hopes that the situation somehow self corrects, finally when all else fails seeking of causes and treatment for the troubling behaviors.

Just as there are resources for those suffering with mental disorders, there are an array of resources specifically designed to assist families in understanding and coping with the mental disorders their family member; its residual effects on the family as well as how to bring the entire family into a state of health.

Counseling and Mental Disorders

Mental Disorders are complex and require a multi-faceted approach to treatment. It usually begins with a complete and thorough psychiatric and physical examination followed by a combination of treatments that can be grouped into four categories:

A.   Physical treatments: Includes medical interventions, dietary changes and in some cases surgery or electroshock therapy.

B.   Psychotherapeutic treatments: Psychotherapy that focuses on emotional-psychological issues; Cognitive and behavior therapies; and teaching of social skills

C.   Community strategies: Engaging community support groups and larger church groups

D.   Spiritual interventions: For those who are believers it is imperative that they receive deliberate spiritual support. There can be considerable support from fellow believers for prayer and reinforcement that there is hope and healing.

Giving affected families members support, education, and when needed counseling can also be of great assistance in treating mental disorders.

An important issue that must be prioritized in treating mental disorders is the occurrence of suicide. Causes of suicide vary greatly from escaping loneliness, attention seeking, hopelessness, pressures including financial, work, academic or work related. Prevention should be of high priority. Counselors must know the potential symptoms of suicide and how to properly intervene. In cases where they cannot, grief and spiritual counseling for surviving family members is vital.

The church has a significant role to play in helping those with Mental Disorders. Jesus' example of compassion, empathy, care and social concern is the model needed to help those who are suffering, often in silence.

References

Section I

Anxiety

WebMD **9 Tips for Anxiety Relief and Management** WebMD
Medical Reference | Reviewed by Joseph Goldberg, MD on June 12,
2017 h ps://www.webmd.com/anxiety-panic/anxiety-Ċps#1

Medical News Today **What are some foods to ease your anxiety?**
by Cathleen Crichton-Stuart | Last reviewed Wed 1 August 2018
Reviewed by Natalie Butler, RD, LD
h ps://www.medicalnewstoday.com/arĊcles/322652.php

HelpGuide **Therapy for Anxiety**
h ps://www.helpguide.org/arĊcles/anxiety/therapy-for-anxiety-
disorders.htm

Depression

Mayo Clinic **Depression and anxiety: Exercises and symptoms**
h ps://www.mayoclinic.org/diseases-condiĊons/depression/in-
depth/depression-and-exercise/art-20046495

Help Guide **Depression Treatment Guide** Authors: Joanna Saisan,
MSW., Melinda Smaiht, M.A, and Jeanne Segal, Ph.D. last updated
June 2019 h ps://www.helpguide.org/arĊcles/depression/
depression-treatment.htm

Healthline **The Effects of Depression in Your Body**
Medically reviewed by Timothy J. Legg, PhD, CRNP on
September 11, 2017 — Written by Ann Pietrangelo and
Kristeen Cherney h ps://www.healthline.com/health/
depression/effects-on-body#1

Anger Management

Healthline **Anger Management Exercises to Help You Stay Calm**
Medically reviewed by Timothy J. Legg, PhD, CRNP on
December 3, 2018 — by Erica Cirino h ps://
www.healthline.com/health/anger-management-exercises

Mayo Clinic **Anger Management: 10 Tips to Tame Your Temper** h ps://www.mayoclinic.org/healthy-lifestyle/adult-health/in-depth/anger-management/art-20045434

Victoria State Government/ Better Health Channel **Anger How It Affects People** Last updated: March 2019 h ps:// www.be erhealth.vic.gov.au/health/healthyliving/anger-how-it-affects-people

Grief
HelpGuide **Coping with Grief and Loss** Authors: Melinda Smith, M.A., Lawrence Robinson and Jeanne Segal, Ph.D. Last updated: June 2019 h ps://www.helpguide.org/arĊcles/grief/coping-with-grief-and-loss.htm

Harvard Health Publishing Harvard Medical School **How to Overcome Grief's Health- Damaging Effects** Published April 2018 h ps:// www.health.harvard.edu/mind-and-mood/how-to-overcome-griefs-health-damaging-effects

Section II

Trauma, Terror, and Terrorism
Summary of Chapter 39, pgs.762-780, Gary R. Collins, PhD., Christian Counseling: A Comprehensive Guide 3rd Edition (Nelson 2007)

Mental Disorders
Summary of Chapter 33, pgs. 633-655, Gary R. Collins, PhD., Christian Counseling: A Comprehensive Guide 3rd Edition (Nelson 2007)

ABOUT THE AUTHOR

Jenee Q. Landrum, PhD is a counselor, teacher, and deliverance minister with more than 30 years in ministry and public service. She is an ordained elder, sought after public speaker, private Christian Counselor and certified Life Coach and Motivational Counselor.

Dr. Landrum's secular work as a crisis counselor and case manager inspired her to focus on mental health solutions for people of faith suffering from spiritual difficulties in conjunction with mental and emotional traumas.

Dr. Landrum holds a B.A., MTh and PhD in Pastoral Care and Counseling. She serves as adjunct professor at ACTSIU/Bethel Bible College, founder of JQ Landrum Ministries and CEO of JenVa Publishing

www.ingramcontent.com/pod-product-compliance
Lightning Source LLC
Chambersburg PA
CBHW070923150426
42812CB00049B/1414